Wha's like us?

Wha's like us?

A HISTORY OF STONEHOUSE

John R. Young

© John R. Young
1996

ISBN 0 9527374 0 X

Published by
John R. Young
01698 792479

Printed by
Cordfall Ltd
0141 332 4640

Dedicated to my father Roderick N. Young for the inspiration and guidance he had given me throughout my life, and to my wife Helen (Murray), for her support in producing this book.

Contents

Introduction	11
The Origins of Stonehouse	13
St. Ninian's Graveyard	15
St. Ninian's Pewter,	17
Communion tokens	
Holy Wells	20
Cat Castle	21
Ringsdale Castle,	22
Kemps Castle	
Double Dykes	23
The Roman Road	24
Mounds & Cairns	25
Cists of Patrickholm	26
The Glesart Stanes	27
The Banks of the Avon	28
The Alexander Hamilton Memorial Park	31
The Flicks	32
The Stanis Weavers	35
(Living Conditions),	38
The But, Cooking, Water, Sanitation, Washing, Lighting, Religion & Politics	
(Working Conditions),	43
The Jacquard Handloom, Spinning, Tambouring, Samplers	
Mining,	45
Canderigg Colliery 1936-1939	
Agriculture	51
Trades	52
The Railway	54
Road Links	57

Stonehousians,	58
Patrick Hamilton, James Hamilton, Gavin Jack,	
Robert Naismith, Archibald Mathie	
The Covenanters	65
The Church after the Reformation,	71
The Parish Church, The Free Church,	
The United Presbyterian Church	
Education	74
Leisure,	79
Adult Recreation, Youth Recreation	
Fairs	83
Musical Entertainment	86
The Pipe Band, The Silver Band, The Male Voice Choir,	
A' the Airts Burns Club	
Stonehouse Hospital	88
The Stanis Witches	91
Hamilton Advertiser Extracts,	93
Tales from the past	
Sandford	101
Politics	103
The War Years,	104
The First World War, The Second World War,	
The reason for the scar	
Modern Stonehouse,	112
The New Town Plan, Stonehouse Heritage Group	
Definition of Place Names	121
Parish Population Changes	
Bibliography	124
List of Illustrations	126
Acknowledgements	128

Foreword

Whatever makes the past, the distant, or the future, predominate over the present, advances us in the dignity of thinking beings.

Dr. Samuel Johnson (1709-1784)

In reading the following pages I have gained the impression of the warp and weft of a woven fabric. The warp, extending throughout the web from end to end, is the author's intense affection for his native Stonehouse and his intimate acquaintance with its history and the beauty of its environs; while the intersecting weft consists of fact and fancy, local lore and oral tradition, personal reminiscences and character sketches. The result is a medley presenting matters of interest to the reader already familiar with the Parish, and offering inducement for others not to lose time in furthering their knowledge of it.

The author has put much into this book above all patience, keen observation and the application of skill in the presentation. He has indeed done a service to those of us who cherish our Parish and wish to preserve for our children the feel, sounds and the magic of the past. Too often we expect the old tales to be passed on and to survive without writing them down. Many of the legends have thus been lost or have faded.

The economic and social development of Stonehouse has, until relatively recent times, depended on local enterprise and initiative. Our interest in the past will serve as a guide to the future. We must not forget that we have one of the oldest parishes in Scotland of great ecclesiastical antiquity.

My own venture into the realms of the past took place when I became curious as to how I had acquired my christian names. Researching back to my grandfather Hugh Dewar Burns, farmer and innkeeper in the Parish of Stonehouse, revealed that he had been christened by and named after the parish minister of that time, the Rev. Hugh Dewar (1794-1861).

There is so much of historical interest in this project to stimulate pride in citizenship and a resolve to make further study. It was an honour and privilege to write this foreword.

H. D. Burns

Hugh Dewar Burns

Wha's like us?

Introduction

Am I an incomer to Stonehouse? I was born and brought up in the village, but my father arrived here in 1954 with his grandmother, Roberta Wylie Lawson (Young), when he was transferred to Stonehouse Hospital suffering from tuberculosis. My early years and school days were spent at 7 Townhead Street, where, with my sisters Roda and Shona, we had the freedom of a large garden and the surrounding countryside to explore.

My father had a great interest in history as I did at school, and our family were great campers and walkers. Through these influences and my parents' guidance, I have in time become interested in our village's history and environment. I never had a natural talent for learning at school I tended to learn, those subjects which I enjoyed the most, such as Scottish history and the Arts. After leaving school I spent three years training in art and design where I learned my trade. This led me in turn to my present employment as a graphic designer for the Education Resource Service in Hamilton. With the vast amount of resources, including an excellent 'Scottish Room', I developed a keen interest in local history.

Around 1989, I was beginning to take an active part in the community, joining the Community Council and the Youth Forum. During my three years with the Youth Forum, I produced, with the help of the children, a magazine called *The Stonehouse Lantern*, in which on occasion I wrote articles of historical interest. With my accumulated research material I helped establish the Stonehouse Heritage Group in 1991, which is now flourishing and playing an ever increasing part in the community. Within the Heritage Group I have used my design experience in the production of our annual exhibitions, and literature on the history of our parish. I have experienced great satisfaction in writing these booklets as they have been well received by the village, especially by the children who have used my research material in their own projects in both primary and secondary schools.

Every week the group receives letters asking for, or providing information from all round the world. Much of my time is spent researching these enquiries and all the information gathered is processed on computer. I felt I had reached a point where I had established enough information to compile a book. This is the end product. Much of the information has been documented previously, but much of the material is new. What I have endeavoured to do is make it as readable and enjoyable as possible, avoiding much of the detail and irrelevance. Throughout my research I have found many inaccuracies and misleading information. I have also been guilty of these on occasion in my booklets. It is often best to research each topic and statement personally as each interpretation of a reference can differ greatly from another. Through visiting my references, I have established a clearer image of the subject I am writing, and often find new suggestions as to how a situation or site has transpired.

Somewhere in the middle of all this I manage to find the time to keep myself fit by long distance running and have also recently become a member of A' the Airts Burns Club, where my wife and I are known as the 'Jacobite Duo'. I have been learning to play the Bhodran, (which my wife Helen, has been regretting buying me as a wedding present ever since) and enjoy traditional folk music to the extent that my wife is fed up with me singing songs with 'Charlie' in them. If you were to ask me politically which party I support, I would have to say 'Independence' for Stonehouse, thus the reason for the book! This has arisen, through my love, interest and memories of a village I believe has a strong, and no doubt eventful future.

The Origins

In prehistoric times the natural place to settle would be by the Avon with its fertile holms and abundance of fish in its rivers, and so it is believed that before the dawn of recorded history on a small mound half a mile to the west of the village probably stood the "standing stones". On this sacred ground stood a monument to the religion of the time run by priests called druids. The word druid means 'knowledge of the oak'. Not only were these men priests but wise men, law makers and law enforcers. The Celts way of life was ruled and governed by Druiadic festivals, tribal law and knowledge passed down only to boys of noble or royal birth. This was learned by heart and never written down. Understandably this is why so little of their lifestyle is known today. Contrary to belief, ceremonies did not take place at the stones, but in the privacy of the woods. Sacrifices tended to be small animals like chickens and occasionally a goat. Human sacrifices were rare and almost always Roman. The stones are thought to be a religious meeting place similar to our churches, hence the expression "let's go to the stanes", a saying still used today which simply means "let's go to church". If there were stones present in the parish it is most likely that it would be a singular or trio of stones as was more popular on the south west coast of Scotland rather than the more commonly thought of circular collection of stones found in the north of Scotland and southern England. The fact that a stone cist was found in St.Ninian's graveyard confirms this site as a place of pagan burial. There can still be seen today, three standing stones at Avonholm overlooking the Avon between Stonehouse and Glassford. It is possible that from the word "Stanes" it has through time been corrupted into the present Stonehouse.

In far off Rome an army was assembling and in the year 55 BC Julius Caesar invaded England bringing it under the rule of the Roman Empire, later invading Scotland in AD 80. By the year AD 142 a wall known as the 'Antonine Wall' had been built between the Clyde in the west and the Forth in the east. Although they tried to invade further north they found the Picts and the Celts a formidable force, especially the Damnii tribe whose domain covered this parish. The Damnii were one of the most powerful and civilised of all the tribes, and whose language may be traced in the names of many of the localities and streams around Stonehouse. This too can be said of the Roman language 'Latin', for instance in the name 'Secaurin' meaning 'home by the riverside', though this word may be from the word 'securing', as in securing the river banks, which was done annually.

After the birth of Christ, Christianity spread throughout the Roman Empire and by AD 300 had become the official religion of the Empire. Around the middle of the fourth century a man called Ninian was born near the Solway and was later converted to Christianity. He travelled to Rome and after a period of study moved to France to continue his instruction in Christianity. His ultimate goal was to bring Christianity to his homeland of Scotland. Legend tells us that he brought earth from 'Candida Casa' (house of white stone, near Whithorn) and with his monks, scattered this on the ancient burial grounds of pagan worship such as the 'stanes' of Stonehouse. It is believed that some of this sacred earth was taken from Stonehouse to consecrate the grounds of the Glassford Kirk cemetery.

Locally Stonehouse is one of the oldest parishes in Scotland and so it is very difficult to trace its origins. It was common to name towns after the first stone house built which was more often a church. Early settlement houses were built with a layered combination of turf and stone or were merely mud cottages. When Ninian preached the gospel on his travels his stonemasonry skills would have been invaluable to him in building his churches.

Robert Naismith wrote of the culminations of the word 'Stonehouse' including Stanes, Stannas and Stanhus. The oldest recorded mentioning of the word appears to be a notice stating that the parish of Stonehouse and the churchyard were to be dedicated in the ninth century to St.Ninian. The earliest records of a landowner in Stonehouse appears about the year 1220, for between the years 1214-49, Sir William (the Fleming) de Douglas of Stanhus appears as a witness to a charter along with Sir Archibald Douglas. The Douglases were the chief landowners of the parish until the reign of James II who endeavoured to destroy the Douglases and install the Hamiltons to the Barony of Stonehouse. Thereafter the proprietors of the parish have been well documented by Naismith and the Statistical Accounts.

'STONE KNOWES', These are burial stones on top of a mound of earth. Knowe is the Scottish version of the word knoll meaning a round hillock or mound. This leads to yet another possibility in the origins of the word Stonehouse. The old kirk graveyard is built on such a mound and it is easy to see how the word can be corrupted into the present Stonehouse. The inscription STAN HOWSE on the pewter plates has a similar sound in its pronunciation.

Whatever the mystery surrounding the origins of the village and its name it is a parish steeped in history and intrigue.

St. Ninian's Graveyard

It is most probable that this was the earliest place of burial within the parish. A stone cist was found within the graveyard some time ago but its date is uncertain, though it may be prehistoric. The old kirk was dedicated to St.Ninian in the 9th century though earlier churches may have been present, probably made from timber. All that remains today is the gable end of a pre-Reformation church and its bell tower. It is believed that Glassford churchyard grounds were consecrated with earth taken from St.Ninian's churchyard. The present remains of Glassford churchyard are almost identical to those that remain in St Ninian's churchyard in Stonehouse. We know the church is pre-Reformation, because restoration work took place in the year 1734, when, in replacing the foundation stone, it was found to be prior to 1560. The view that the kirk still today commands is one of the most beautiful on the Avon valley.

The old kirk appeared to still be in use in the late seventeenth century, as James Robertson of Hazeldean was reported to have affixed a paper in defence of the Covenanters to the door of the parish kirk around 1680.[1] Stonehouse has a strong connection with the Covenanters. Many men including James Hamilton of Kittymuir and Robert Findlay from the parish were executed for their beliefs. Probably the best known Covenanter to most of us is James Thomson of Tanhill who fell at the battle of Drumclog in 1679. He was later buried at the old graveyard in Stonehouse where his tombstone can still be seen. The stone was later renewed in the form of a tablestone in 1832.

Over the years the graveyard has been the target for vandalism with over two hundred and fifty grave stones being pushed over. This, however, is not 'a sign of the times' as some think, as this sort of crime has been going on for over a century as this extract from the *Hamilton Advertiser* of March 1882 reveals:

> *On Wednesday it was discovered that some person had maliciously entered the graveyard and thrown down a tombstone erected sometime ago by Mr George Cuthbertson, Green Street. The coping was broken off and damaged, and the top ornament had been taken away. As no trace of it can be found, the case has been given into the hands of the police for investigation. It is supposed the depredators must have done the mischief between Tuesday night and Wednesday morning.*

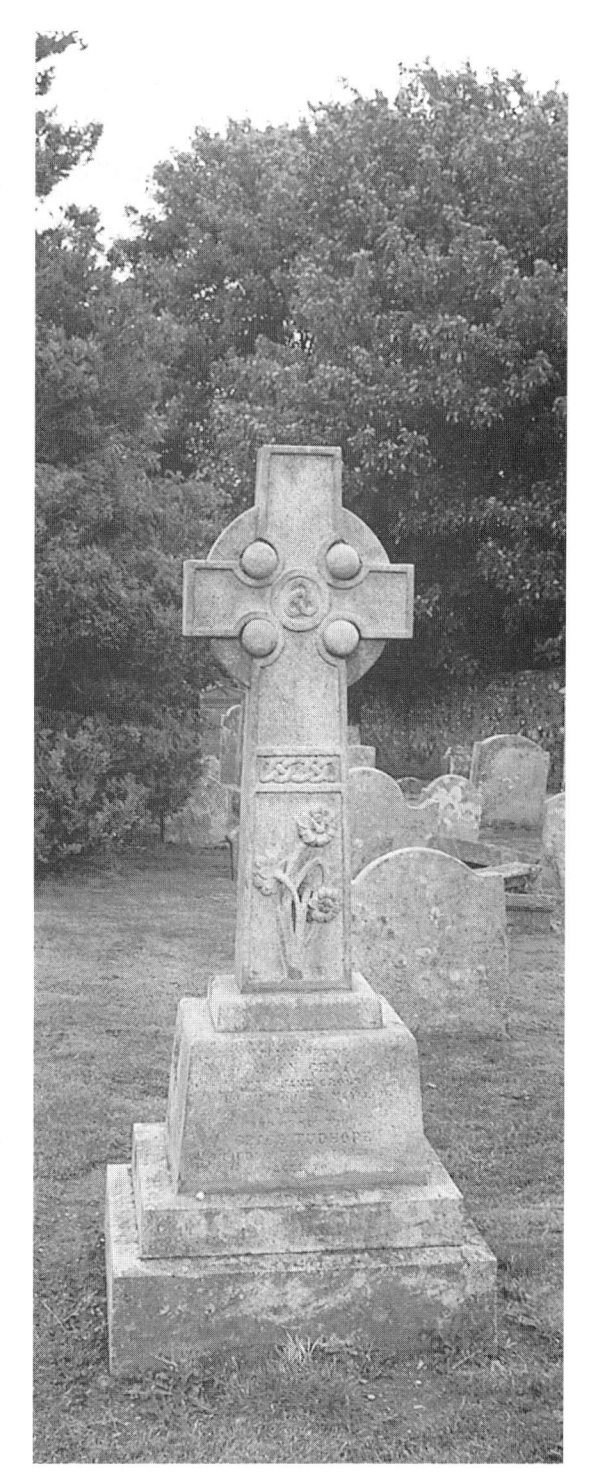

Reference: 1 **Stonehouse, Traditional and Historical**

However there is light on the horizon. Stonehouse Heritage Group initiated a restoration and preservation project to raise and clean as many of the stones as possible. This proved successful and the Heritage Group is now looking to repair damage caused by the natural elements to the gable end of the bell tower. The group hopes that by making the community more aware of their historical background, future generations may learn to appreciate and protect their environment.

The remains of the old kirk are remembered in the lines:[1]

> *Hail! ruined remnant of a Church*
> *Old silent belfry grey*
> *With scars of age; the tooth of time*
> *Has gnawed all else away*
>
> *Thy voice speaks to the thoughtful mind;*
> *This ancient house of prayer*
> *Revives anew those hallowed scenes*
> *Of beauty, rich and rare.*

Reference: 1 **Hamilton Advertiser**

St. Ninian's Pewter

Pewter was once common place. Now it turns up in nearly every antique shop, the finest specimens fetching large sums. Most Scottish pewter, however, has emigrated. Old Scottish pewter is generally of better than average quality in the workmanship and metal, is comparatively scarce. Dented, worn or leaky pieces were valuable as scrap and were melted down to make new; and the country did not have plentiful supplies of tin, one of the main ingredients.

The most famous and highly prized Scottish items are tappit hens: vessels of elegant design. Most tappit hens hold one Scottish pint, which was the equivalent of three Imperial pints. The earliest known to have survived dates from about 1669 but most are from between about 1750-1850.

Plates which are Scottish may be unrecognised, masquerading as English because they lack the marks that should distinguish them. Hard up congregations bought pewter communion cups, wine flagons, bread plates and offering plates and the name of the church was sometimes engraved on them. Church pewter has survived in greater quantity than household pewter because it was carefully kept and little used.

Pewter tarnishes with time and with exposure to air becomes scaly. Its surface may become blemished with pock marks and small bubbling eruptions which can never be cured. Newly made and highly polished pewter looks like silver, especially at a distance with indoor light. That was one reason why people bought it. Sometimes the makers helped along the deception by putting on their products marks which looked like the hallmarks on silver.

Pewter declined as better materials were devised. Iron with a coating of tin, called white iron, was a strong competitor from about 1725. A better imitation of silver was invented in the 1740s—Sheffield plate, which is copper between two thin sheets of silver. Tea ousted beer as the people's everyday drink from the beginning of the nineteenth century onwards; and tea does not taste right in pewter. Pottery and porcelain became comparatively cheap in the second half of the eighteenth century and hit the pewter traders badly.

Within an old chest at St.Ninian's Church were found two pewter communion plates, three pewter flagons and several hundred communion coins. The largest flagon was made by partners Robert Graham and James Wardrope from Glasgow around the year 1790 only seven years after the end of the American Wars of Independence. Both Robert and James were obviously in favour of American freedom as their makers mark shows a sailing ship with the words "SUCCESS TO THE UNITED STATES OF AMERICA" inscribed round the ship. Another of the pewter flagons was made by J.Wylie of Glasgow around the year 1840. Both these vessels are prized 'tappit hens'. The third flagon is highly ornamented with the makers mark PA & S inscribed, but little is known of its origins.

The two pewter plates are some eighteen inches in diameter, one of which has the words 'STAN HOWSE KERK', with Stonehouse inscribed clearly in two separate words. Further round the rim there is inscribed IM above the letters AD. Initially it was believed that this represented a date (AD 999) but after the plates were analysed by Kelvingrove Museum it was thought that this marking was either a makers mark or a ministers initials. Pewter was not in use in Scotland as early as our first assumptions, though the Romans were known to use pewter earlier than this but to a far greater standard of material and quality of craftsmanship. I initially disregarded the idea that the mark was a minister's initials as there were no ministers with the initials IM as far back as 1560. But after researching the pewter flagons, which I was able to date fairly accurately, I found no mention of the makers mark in connection with the plates. What I did find however was that a 'J' shown on a makers mark in the eighteenth century and earlier was shown as an 'I'. Just as Indiana Jones tried to cross the stone tablet causeway in *The Last Crusade* trying to step on the tablets that spelled Jehovah, I was faced with the same problem. Like him I tried to spell it as it sounded with a 'J' but to no avail.

With this information I again traced previous ministers to find 'James Muirhead' who was ordained on "25th Sept. Anno Domini 1760". This date not only coincided with the flagons, but also with the communion coins dating to 1767, all of which were found in the chest. It would seem that James Muirhead ministered in the old kirk and may have been the first minister in the parish church built in New Street in 1771-2. The plates are almost certainly communion plates but through time have decayed considerably. Unfortunately pewter is difficult to preserve and nearly impossible to repair. Such is the condition of the Stonehouse plates.

Communion Tokens

Churches in Scotland used to issue worthy and godly folk with tokens to allow them to take communion. These communion tokens are inexpensive to collect and give an insight into long-dead customs.

Tokens are small discs—up to one and a half inches across, and are generally made of lead, but also sometimes very rarely, of brass, tin, copper, iron and leather. They are square, oblong, round, triangular, or in various other shapes. Each coin had to be unmistakably designed or imprinted for a particular parish or congregation, to prevent imposters from getting to the communion table. Tokens thus, have the initial letters of the parish, or its full name, or the minister's initials or a picture of the church.

Communion was usually held about once a year, but in some places only once in seven or nine years, from the end of the seventeenth century until about 1750. The people and the churches wanted to be sure they were ready for the sacrament.

Tokens got worn out or lost, or if they had the minister's name, became obsolete when a minister moved. They were treated with almost superstitious reverence because of their connection with the sacrament. Old ones were on occasion buried beneath the pulpit; or they were melted to make new.

The makers were local blacksmiths, plumbers or pewterers. Punches or dyes were used to imprint the design; or molten metal was poured into stone moulds; or a copper coin was hammered out and the metal was crudely engraved by hand. Sadly, this tradition died out towards the end of the Victorian period when printed cards came into use.

Stonehouse was no exception in producing communion tokens. The earliest recorded token is from the year 1736 when John Scott was the parish minister. The next coin is very similar in design from the year 1767 when James Muirhead presided until 1780. The coins of 1824 and 1835 date to a time when the coins were slowly going out of circulation. From 1821 to 1829 David Wilkie was ministering in Stonehouse as was Hugh Dewar from 1820 until 1860. The United Secession Church which is inscribed on the 1835 communion coin, later joined the Church of Scotland in 1956.

Holy Wells

Scotland has an abundance of holy wells and Stonehouse is no exception. Four holy wells are found within the parish and numerous other wells supply the water needs of the village. Stonehouse appears to be technically an island, surrounded by rivers and burns making it impossible to leave the village without crossing water, thus there is no lack of supply to the wells. Holy wells are of pagan origin, from a time when there were many superstitions surrounding water. Pilgrims and Christians from all over the surrounding country would flock to try their healing properties or administer Christian baptisms, as was probably the case at St. Ninian's well. This well like the old kirk church and churchyard, was dedicated to St. Ninian. It has over the centuries been corrupted into Ringan Well and to Ring Well. Today all that remains is a hole covered with stone slabs, filled with rubbish, between the farm of Eastmains and the old kirk. Cows now graze here.

Situated on the banks of the Avon on the lands of Patrickholm lies St. Patrick's well, famous for its healing properties in curing tuberculosis and skin diseases. This may just be a coincidence but Stonehouse Hospital was originally built in 1896 to provide care and treatment for sufferers of tuberculosis and other related diseases. This well, like so many others was dedicated to another preacher of Christianity. St. Patrick is said to have spread the gospel throughout this area including Dalserf and, like Ninian, his name appears throughout the country. This sulphurous spring can still be seen today trickling through a stratum of rock and cascading down the gorge. Its smell and white colouring are easily identifiable. Ordnance survey maps record this as a physic well.

St. Antony's Well was a prominent well in its time, also known as Brackenhill Well, situated not a great distance from Spittal House which was formerly a hospital and a convent built in 1723. Spittal or 'spittle', in a dictionary is described as a hospital for foul diseases. The well can still be found today surrounded by a small stone wall one and a half feet high and about four feet square. Unfortunately, through boring during the New Town survey the well has long since dried up. It is thought that Antony came from a wealthy family and spoke only his native language which was that of the ancient Egyptians. He was known as a carer of the poor, patron and protector of the lower animals. The well which was dedicated to him was notable for being high in iron content and known for curing diseases particularly those affecting horses. It was believed that horses were taken to drink at the spring and sometimes water was carried a considerable distance for the same purpose. In the summer of 1994, the Heritage Group carried out a restoration project on the well which has over the past century suffered through vandalism and the elements of nature. It is hoped that this will be the first of many projects of this nature, preserving our ever decaying history.

St. Laurence's Well rises from the Watston Burn at Chapel Farm where an ancient chapel was formerly built, dedicated to St. Laurence, thus he is guardian of this well. Little is known of this well or its medicinal powers. St. Laurence himself was known to be a deacon and martyr of Rome, carer of the destitute, helpless and sick. Today the well is home to various water fowl on Chapel Farm.

Cat, Cot, Coat Castle

Not much is known of this mysterious castle which once enchanted the banks of the Avon. Resting on a precipitous cliff face, the castle or 'Keep' as it should be known was home to the Hamiltons in the year AD 1500. The failure of Edward I to impose lasting peace in Scotland brought about three centuries of border warfare. With the constant destruction and changing possession of castles it proved to be time consuming and expensive to constantly maintain and defend great fortresses thus the fourteenth and fifteenth centuries saw the evolution of a type of 'keep' or 'tower house' more appropriate to the reduced resources of the defenders. This stone structure was both fireproof and capable of being defended should the castle be stormed. Basically it was a type of fortified house rather than a castle. In Ireland and Scotland the keeps tended to be smaller than their English counterparts, a compromise between comfort and security where the sudden raid was feared more than the prolonged siege. The basic type of keep was either square or rectangular rising through three or more storeys enclosing hall, chamber, kitchen, chapel and final place of refuge. Cot Castle was probably very similar to the keep (tower house) within Craignethan Castle which is thought to date from the fifteenth century. Cot Castle is noted in Bartholomew's Castles Map of Scotland as a Keep and in 1836 there were said to be remains still visible.

In the 1937 *Statistical Account of Stonehouse* mention is made of Cot Castle in the following extract:

> *Among the documents discovered in 1887 in the Hamilton Chamberlain's office, is a notarial instrument, narrating that in terms of a charter granted by himself, Alexander Hamilton of Catcastell, passed to the one-mark of Woodland and the half-merk land of Brownland, lying in the barony of Stanehouse and the sheriffdom of Lanark and there gave sasine of these lands with his own hands to James Wynzet, his heirs and assignees in usual form, 29th January 1511-12.*

Near the ruins of Cot Castle, limekilns were opened to extract the lime which is abundant in the area in the early nineteenth century. All that remains are a pair of single-draw limekilns set into the bank with spherical arched draw holes and projecting buttresses.

In the late 1940s a famous Clydesdale stallion was stabled at Cot Castle farm. Many people may still remember the stallion being led through the village to serve mares on the surrounding farms. Cot Castle farm was later built on this site but fell into disrepair and was abandoned at the end of the 1970s.

Ringsdale Castle

Like Cot Castle, Ringsdale was probably a Scottish 'keep' rather than a castle. It once stood high on the roof of the Avon gorge overlooking the winding waters of the river. The name of the castle possibly derives from the ancient language of the Britons, Rhyn, signifying a promontory or hill. The word has been corrupted in pronunciation to Ringsdale. Today all that remains of the castle are large stone blocks that have fallen from the summit of the gorge to the river banks. Even the romantically located Glenavon Cottage which once stood next to Ringsdale has vanished to an enchanted memory of the past, though a small corner of its walls still stands to mark its resting place. On a map of 1838, there is marked a mill known as Cloxy Mill (Clocksy, 1864) near the remains of Ringsdale Castle. Today there are still ruins of the mill to be seen on the banks of the Avon, but no records of its origins.

Castles appear to be abundant in this area. On the outskirts of the parish can be found the sites of Allanton, Brocket, Plotcock, Glassford and Darngaber castles.

Kemps Castle

During my research into castles within the parish I came across 'Kemp Castle' in several Statistical Accounts and Robert Naismith's book which state that one of the names given to Cot Castle in the past had been Kemp Castle. Robert Naismith refers to Bleau's map of 1596 as his reference. I initially took this information for granted and used it in my booklet 'The Historic Sites of Stonehouse'. As I have found in the past, it is often wise to research the subject matter personally, as when I consulted the map I found in fact that there were two 'Kat Castles' and Kemp Castle where we more commonly know as Castlehill. Castlehill, as we now know it, lies about six hundred feet above sea level, commanding an excellent panoramic view of the surrounding countryside. In 1710 Castlehill belonged to Lord Lee who later moved to Cambusnethan House in the Clyde Valley. The site was said to be ruinous and it is possible that it then merely became known as Castlehill. In the Scots dialect kemp means; one who fights in single combat or a professional fighter, a variety of potato or a stalk and seed head of rib grass. It is possible that this castle had been an ancestral home of the Kemp family, of whom there was a large concentration in the Hamilton area at one time. Hamilton still retains the name by way of 'Kemp Street' off Quarry Street. The name, however, is more commonly associated with Aberdeenshire.[1]

There were two Kat Castles on Bleau's map, one of which we know to be present one located at the head of Strathaven Road. The second appears to be in the region of High Longridge (Langrigg) farm and is indicated merely as 'Kat Castle B'. What the B signifies is uncertain, though it may have been a previous siting of the castle. High Lanrigg would appear to have been an ideal location for the castle, resting six hundred feet above sea level.

Reference: 1 Black's **Surnames of Scotland**

Double Dykes

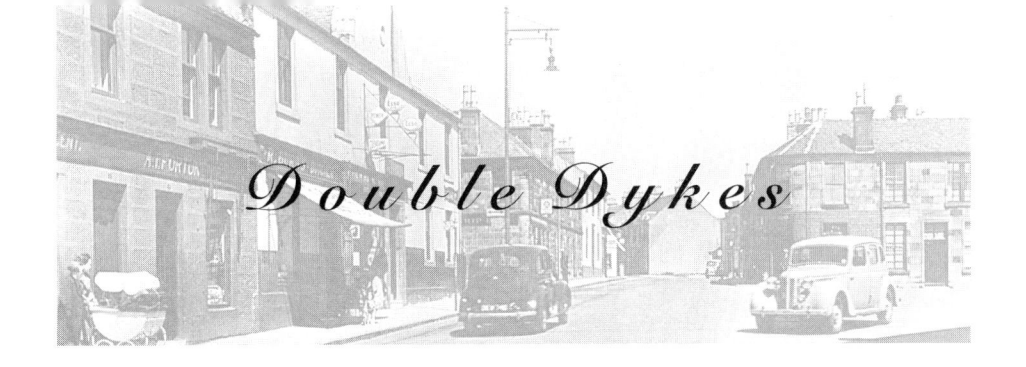

At the eastern side of the parish, south of Ringsdale Castle the River Avon and the Cander Water converge on the steep banks of the Avon Gorge. The tapering piece of land between these streams is known as Double Dykes. This site is adjacent to an old stone quarry in the Avon gorge, hence the name of the right of way leading to this site known as 'Quarry road end'. About a quarter of a mile from the apex, two or three ramparts and walls are viewed from north to south in a semi-circular fashion, forming defences for the base of the triangle. In some areas the walls can still be seen and in others broken down due to much of the stone being taken away for building purposes nearby. The origins of these defences are uncertain,

Naismith suggests it may have been a Roman fort. It may well have been a fortlet, a smaller version of a fort designed to house no more than fifty to eighty men in one or two barrack blocks. Fortlets usually had a single gate through the rampart, with a timber tower above, and one or two ditches beyond. Fortlets are found in Scotland at intermediate points along major roads, or at river crossings. The fort may even be older dating to the Iron Age. Whatever its origins, its defences must have been nigh impregnable. In 1972 the Royal Commission of Ancient and Historical Monuments of Scotland surveyed the site, but found no internal structures behind the dykes. However, lines can be seen at certain times of the year and suggest that a more detailed survey may be required to ascertain the origins of this historical site.

A fortalice is 'a small outwork of fortification or fortress'. Naismith states "The old fortalice of Cander commanded an excellent position of the banks of Cander Water, and it seems to have been in decay in 1700". He further points out that this fortalice at Cander stood near to the town and belonged to a branch of the Hamilton Family. I can find no recordings of any castle or fort on the Cander. I am uncertain if Naismith is refering to Double Dykes, or possibly the site of the present Candermains Farm, which is close to the village and has an excellent view of the Cander.

The Roman Road

In AD 80 Governor Cnaeus Julius Agricola led a Roman army of twenty thousand men into Scotland establishing forts between the Clyde and the Forth. To control this new frontier the Romans set about building a network of roads. In Scotland the route of the roads were determined by the contours of the land along valleys still used today by the modern rail and road networks. Roman roads are found today by their raised mounds in the countryside, by observation on maps, farm-tracks, field boundaries, placenames indicating roads, from the air and quarry pits used in their building. When an excavation of a Roman road takes place, a lower stratum of large cobbles are found, some six metres across topped with small stones and gravel and flanked often by drainage gullies. Roman roads are well known for their straightness, but due to the complexity of Scotland's geographical contours these roads were often not straight, especially when following a river. Distances along the roads were marked by milestones, of which only one survives in Scotland, from Ingliston. Many more may lie undiscovered.

Stonehouse can lay claim to having part of the Roman road system running through the parish. A stretch of this road can be seen at Dykehead by taking the road up Sidehead Road to Avondyke Training Centre. Two field boundaries south of Dykehead Farm lie just beyond the training centre. Go left through a metal field gate and follow the fence downhill to another gate. From there onwards the raised mound is viewed from the left edge of the field. The embankment stands half a meter high, and can be followed on foot for two kilometres to Gill farmhouse. A slight ridge is all that remains of this causeway near the farm of Tanhill. The Roman road is situated on the highest point of the parish, peaking at seven hundred and thirty five feet in the area of Dykehead. Unfortunately, the road has suffered through drainage, ploughing and fencing, and by 1836 evidence of existence had become confined to the Greenburn area. In 1938 paving in the form of large stones was still to be seen, south of Chapel Farm.

In 1836 came the opening of the Edinburgh to Ayr turnpike road with access to Canderside toll. The Roman road, like the turnpike road appeared to have been built from Ayr to Edinburgh as a supply route passing through the forts at Castledykes and Allanton near Loudon Hill. The road was formerly known as the 'Deil's causey' as those of superstitious beliefs believed the Devil had a hand in its making.

Mounds & Cairns

There exist three sites of interest within the parish which are clearly indicated on ordnance survey maps either as a mound or cairn. The first is a mound lying on the line of the Roman road along the Udston Road a quarter of a mile on the right from Chapel Farm heading west. Following the line of trees for approximately sixty metres to the right of which the Roman road takes its course you will find a distinct circular patch of land some ten metres in diameter. The mound is flat now, possibly due to the marshy soft ground or agricultural land improvements. The ground on which the mound rests is distinctly different from the surrounding land as little seems to grow on this patch apart from heather, low growing grasses and two or three young birches. In the centre of the mound there is a little water retention. May this mound have been a burial mound (possibly Roman) like that at Mount Pisgah on the lands of West Mains?

A cairn can be found by taking a left at Fairy Burn Bridge from Sandford towards Tweediehall. A monument stands to the right, a quarter of a mile from the road towards the River Avon, dedicated to the memory of James Whyte and his wife Ann Kerr Bell. To the left of this monument a tree row can be followed towards the river where, two hundred yards away, you will find the remains of a cairn. The cairn is oval in shape, seventeen by seven metres, but this may be due to ploughing over the centuries. The cairn, as shown on the ordnance survey map, leads us to believe that at one time a heap of stones existed on this point indicating a grave or place of burial. No stones are now present on this site, but from viewing the position of the cairn from the map it is clear to see that some kind of structure once existed here. In Robert Naismith's book it is mentioned that "an unopened tumulus (burial mound) is said to exist on the farm of Tweedie". This cairn is most probably the one mentioned. Whether or not anything does remain is unlikely, but until proper excavations of these sites take place, who can tell?

In 1834 a farmer from Westmains (possibly Robert Dykes) was draining an area of land known as Mount Pisgah (near Cot Castle) when he came across a cairn apparently curbed with large stones. In clearing the stones he found a rich black mould metres deep in which lay ancient tumulus and a great many urns all perfectly preserved and ornamented in flowers and figures. The urns were thought to have been made from a light coloured clay and contained pieces of burnt bone, ashes and charred wood. The present whereabouts of these treasures are unknown. In Rev. Hugh Dewar's *Statistical Account* he states, "There have been other tumuli found in the parish, particularly one at the upper end of it; which, some years ago, was ransacked to the centre, and a number of urns found therein".

Just outside the parish boundary there exists an excellent example of a cairn approximately two miles from Canderside Toll on the Blackwood Road known as Cairncockle. In a field three hundred yards to the left after the road leading to Overwood you will find the half circle remains of a cairn measuring about twenty nine metres in diameter with the outer edge of the circle dropping half a metre and being nine metres in width. The surviving segment is crossed by an entrance causeway eight metres in wide. The cairn is halved by a fence running straight through the middle and on the other side is the M74 motorway embankment.

Cists of Patrickholm

In the autumn of 1947 four prehistoric burial sites of the Middle Bronze Age were discovered at the Patrickholm sand quarry. They were found on the west side of the River Avon, four hundred and twenty feet above sea level near the Larkhall Viaduct. The site was found when workmen at Patrickholm digging and loosening sand, came upon some large stone slabs of a cist (stone coffin). Cist number one was about five feet below ground level and measured about five feet in length. Inside the cist were two fragments of human bones, part of a skull, part of the lower end of a femur of an adult and a food vessel. The urn, which is in excellent condition, measures about four and a half inches in height and is highly ornamented. Six to eight feet from the first burial site a number of pieces of cremated bones of humans were found, but no cist. The bones were thought to have been from a youth between twelve and twenty and a young adult. Amongst the bones and the sand a small piece of flint was found. An unusually small cist measuring two feet by one foot was uncovered full of cremated bones. Like the cist mentioned before it was formed with stone slabs. It too had a great number of bones of at least four individuals, one adult, a younger adult and two children seven to twelve years of age. Among the finds within the cist were a small flint flake, a piece of ironstone, a stone bead and three human bone beads, all cylindrical and probably remnants of a necklace. A third cist of about four feet in length was discovered when accidently broken open by sand diggers with their picks and spades without realising what it was. A second food vessel was found within, again highly ornamented probably using a toothcomb. Inside the vessel were a well preserved molar, one incisor crown and pure brown sand. Also found within the vessel were bone fragments and a small piece of flint. This excavation is particularly interesting because family groups are rare in Bronze Age cists. The date of this site can be estimated at around 2000 BC. The urns found at the Patrickholm site were donated to the National Museum of Antiquities in Edinburgh by the owner of the quarry at that time, Mr McNeil Hamilton.[1]

The ruins of Patrickholm House still stand near the site of the cists, though continuing land improvements may put an end to the house where many past landlords of Stonehouse once resided.

Reference: **1 Proceedings of the Society of Antiquaries of Scotland** *1948*

The Glesart Stanes

Although these stones are just outside our parish boundary in the parish of Glassford, they cannot go without a mention. The 'stones of St.Ninian's' probably resembled these stones in many ways. It is possible that other stones may have stood throughout the surrounding area, but through land improvements these would have long disappeared, lost in time. The 'Glesart Stanes' lie near Avonholm by the Avon, on a hill surrounded by a cluster of trees including oak and holly. These two trees are of particular interest. Oak was the most sacred of trees to the pagan religion said to have the powers from fending off lightning to curing toothache. The word druid means 'knowledge of the oak'. Holly too was used to keep out evil influences.

The stones stand about six feet apart, three feet high, three feet broad and made of sandstone. Two have their backs to the east and the third, not parallel to the others, has its back to the south-east.[1] There is no indication of a circle, as mentioned before. It is more common in this area of Scotland for standing stones to be either on their own or in a trio of stones. There are vertical grooves on two of the stones, while the centre stone has a cup mark, below which is a faint circle, one foot in diameter. They stand on a long, narrow strip of land with low earthen walls on either side. The stones give a wonderful panoramic view of the river Avon and Stonehouse.

You will find the graves of the Struthers of Avonholm buried on this spot along with their pet dogs Blanche and Heidi. This place obviously held fond memories and it was a comfort to the family for them to have chosen it as their final resting place. The purpose of the stones themselves, we can only guess. If only to remind us of our pagan ancestors they stand in peace untouched by the progress of time in an ever changing environment. In the tranquillity of the Avon Valley who is to say the stones won't endure another two thousand years.

Reference: 1 **Glassford the Kirk and the Kingdom**

The Banks of the Avon

The Avon is one of the most endearing and beautiful of all the rivers in Scotland, an inspiration to many a painter's palette and poet's imagination. The River Avon flows through the parish from its source in Ayrshire through the parishes of Strathaven, Glassford, Stonehouse, Dalserf and eventually into the Clyde a mile east of Hamilton. The river is still reckoned to be one of the best trouting streams in Scotland. Salmon used to be plentiful until about 1816 when the mill-dam at Millheugh was raised to procure a more consistent water supply for the mills, thus the salmon were unable to leap the dam. The Linthaugh Bridge which spans the Avon was built in the late eighteenth century to replace the bridge swept away in the floods of 1771. The County and local landowners paid for the new bridge. This and many other bridges were built by Irish immigrants during an era of road building and communication improvements. From Hamilton to Stonehouse an almost uninterrupted range of rocks overhangs the river on both sides, the summits of which are covered with natural wood of ash, birch, oak, elm and many more. The bed of the river in places is congested with large areas of rock which have fallen from the strata, often obstructing the natural flow of the water's passage.

At least three shale mines can be found on the banks of the Avon along the gorge face near Ritchies Dam. These mines were said to have been worked by monks (possibly from Lesmahagow) and later used to extract oil from shale at the oil works nearby. The mines can still be accessed, but this is not advisable as they are low roofed, dark and a labyrinth of tunnels lie within. These mines were also worked to extract coal during the general strike of 1926. It is said there exists a tunnel travelling under the Avon to the north bank, and that a large cave with luminous stalactites hang down from above. This cave is said to be accessed through one of the shale mines.

The Avon has many tributaries which in themselves have a natural beauty and interest. The largest of these is the Kype Water which flows through the hamlet of Sandford. In its course to the Avon it forms a cascade of some fifty feet at St.Helen's Old Mill, better known as the Spectacle E'e Mill. The origins of the name are uncertain but the following extract from *The Larkhall & Stonehouse Gazette* is the popular and romantic version of how the mill came by its name. This theory, however, is questionable, as photographic evidence from a later date, clearly shows the mill in good working order.

> *It is said that long, long ago the miller of Spectacle E'e was prosperous and content. But he was also stubborn and haughty. And as he became a miller in so romantic a spot, he had a lovely daughter who was the apple of his eye. She also delighted the eye of a youth in the hamlet up the stream, but the miller would have none of him. And the youth plotted revenge. One day, towards noon, the people working the fields saw smoke and flames leap up through the trees at the waterside. The mill was on fire! When the flames died down, only the wall remained, but it is not known whether the miller perished or that the youth and the maid were afterwards wed. But the tale was told that, in the night, the spurned suitor had climbed the thatched roof of the mill and fixed by their legs, a pair of spectacles so that, when the sun beat fiercest on the thatch, the lens caught the rays and concentrated them to a burning pin-point on the dry and warm straw. When the flame burst he was far from the mill and so had an alibi. That's how the mill got its name "Spectacle E'e".*

Equally enthralling is the Cander Water, a stream rising from the Parish of Lesmahagow, some six miles to the meetings of the waters at the Fairies Rock, where it is said fairies would come out after dark and dance the night through. Access to the Cander is extremely difficult from the Avon. It can be accessed from Double Dikes (Dykes) down the Cander gorge but it is not advised for the faint hearted. The easiest route when reaching the water is direct through the water. This stretch of water is not deep but there are many blockages of fallen debris which make passage either way a little more difficult. The feeling of seclusion and silence in this gorge is breathtaking, as is the wild garlic, abundant in late spring.

Spanning the Cander you can find Woodlands Bridge built in 1827 by Thomas Telford when the Edinburgh to Ayr turnpike road was first established. Situated up river on the Cander is the remains of Cander grain mill. Formerly powered by water driven machinery, the mill was converted to electricity in 1957. Still seen today is the wheel which drove the drive shaft to the Candermains grain mill, above. Further upstream to this site a hydraulic ram was situated, pumping drinking water from a well to Candermains. The pumping action of the hydraulic ram and the sound that it made became referred to as the 'devils hammer'. If the water is followed towards its source you will encounter the site of the former sandstone quarry at Overwood. Following the Cander Water from Overwood you will come to Gill Bridge where a mill formerly stood. Unfortunately, fire reduced it to ruins in 1879.

There are no lochs in the parish but there was at one time at Goslington, a large area of marsh which supported many water fowl including wild geese and ducks. The Avon in its natural setting is a haven for many birds such as tawny owls, mallards, dippers, cormorants and the occasional kingfisher, one of which was spotted near the Linthaugh Bridge recently. In the Cander gorge there exists a dippers nest that has resided on the hanging rock face for at least sixty years and has been used by generations of dippers. Wildlife is abundant if you know where to look. Deer, mink, badgers and even the otter has returned to the seclusion of these waters. In its often tropical appearance the Avon gorge supports many rare plant species such as Herb Paris and the Lesser Wintergreen. Robert Naismith, a keen botanist, was eager for children to explore and learn from the many interesting and educational elements found within their environment.

> *To train the youth to know the wild flowers of the district in which they reside would be an interesting, instructive, and beneficial method of imparting additional zest into their holiday rambles, and would leave sunny memories in their minds for all future time.*
>
> Robert Naismilh 1885

Researching through old maps of the district, it appears that in 1768 the River Avon, at the Horsepool had a diversion cutting directly across the land. This may have been a man made diversion, in connection with the mill situated at the Horsepool.

Even today the Avon has survived the advance of progress and retains the beauty and character it has enjoyed throughout the centuries. The Avon and Cander gorge has only recently established itself as one of only fourteen sites of 'extra special scientific interest' in Scotland. A site of European status, this priority habitat must be maintained and preserved for future generations to study and enjoy.

Alexander Hamilton Memorial Park

The village's public park is due to the generosity of a former native of Stonehouse, Alexander Hamilton. He was born and brought up in the village and later made his fortune as head of the Victoria Carpet Company in Kidderminster and later making Khaki for the troops in the Great War. It was his wish that he could leave something for the village that he visited annually and loved so dearly. Thus the council were left the task of finding a suitable site. After much discussion and argument a ten acre site was purchased for £500 from the land of Holm Farm. Many people thought a flatter area would be more appropiate and others even thought Mr Hamilton would have been better spending his money on a factory for Stonehouse.

On 30th May 1925 Alexander Hamilton fullfilled his dream and presented the park, bandstand and fountain to his native town. He died four years later.

The bandstand was bought by Fourth District Council from Glasgow District Council in 1924. It formerly stood in Kelvingrove Park, built for the Scottish National Exhibition of 1911. The bandstand was the venue for many bands from all over Scotland, including our own Silverband. There once stood a bandstand on the banks of the Avon near the viaduct, but there is no evidence of it today.

In 1933 the famous chute was installed, said to be the longest in Scotland, if not Europe, at the time. It was opened by Councillor Thomas Wilson, but sadly was dismantled in August 1967 because it was considered too dangerous. Councillor Wilson was at the park again to open the tennis courts, putting green and pavillion in the early 30s. When Sir Harry Lauder visited the park in August 1942, he said, "It's a bonnie park; yin o' the nicest I've ever been in, an' something Stonehoose folk should be rale proud o' ".

There was formerly a nine hole golf course at the Holm Farm. Constructed in 1910, it was opened in 1912. During the war years it was partly cultivated and was abandoned. Despite the recent neglect of the park it still overlooks one of the most spectacular views of the Avon valley.

The immense pillars of the viaduct that overshadow the river Avon are fond memory of the railway. Constructed in 1904 by the Arrol Brothers, for the Caledonian Railway, it was dismantled for scrap in 1984. In its time the viaduct was the longest viaduct in Scotland. During the late eighteenth century and to the latter end of the nineteenth there was an influx of Irish immigrants to Stonehouse, especially to Boghall Street. These men were greatly responsible for much of the road and bridge building around the area.

The Flicks

Directly across from the old parish church in New Street stands the village's first picture house, built around December 1914, and now the premises of 'Top Grade Windows'. Known as 'The Palace', the cinema was designed by Victor Wilson, seating six hundred. The cinema was under the management of Harry Kimm, who organised not only the film shows but also variety entertainment such as Harman, the dancing musician and the local Silverband. Serials such as *Perils of Pauline* and films *Red Circle*, *The Black Box* and *The Master Key* are said to have been among the first shown there. In October 1915, a twelve year old boy from Stonehouse was charged with breaking and entry. The judge in condemning the boy's action, blamed the picture house, which the boy was said to frequent, stating; "He saw how it was done". The Palace was sold at auction for £1060 in March 1918.

It wasn't until January 1937 that the 'Rex' was opened in Argyle Street by the owner, John Edward Sheeran. The picture house was furnished with a chandelier and mahogany panel fittings, including a staircase, from the German ship *Homeric*. The newspaper extract below gave a report on the opening of the cinema.

> January 23rd 1937
> **NEW CINEMA'S FIRST NIGHT**
> *Full homage was done to what can be genuinely termed Lanarkshire's King of picture houses, appropriately named 'The Rex', when it was opened on Thursday night, and a crowded house appreciated and admired this splendidly fitted up structure. Roomily seated to accommodate 750 persons, what was once the concert hall of the* Homeric, *has been transformed into one of the finest cinemas for its size in and no doubt out of the county, and Mr Sheeran may indeed feel proud of the achievement. Film fans will find nothing left to be desired regarding sound equipment and the F.I. (Film Industry) outfit has to be heard to be appreciated. No doubt many will avail themselves at an early opportunity to go, to hear and see what has been a long felt want in the village, and which now having become such a splendid reality deserves every encouragement.*

Launched as *Columbus* on December 17th 1913, in Danzig, construction was held up during World War I and was not completed until 1920. After the Second World War the town of Danzig was renamed Gdansk when it was reclaimed by Poland. The *Homeric* is said to have been built for the Kaiser in the expectation of him winning the First World War. Ceded to Britain in 1919 she was sold to the White Star Line and renamed the *Homeric*. Weighing 34,351 tons she was refitted and completed by 1922 by Harland and Wolff. Her maiden voyage was on February 24th 1922, sailing from Southampton to New York as a cruise ship. The *Homeric* had the distinction of being the largest twin screw ship in the world at the time of her launch but unfortunately she was too slow at eighteen knots for Atlantic crossings and thus was refitted again to improve her speed and convert her coal burners to oil. In 1924 it was decided that her third class passenger capacity was too large and deemed unprofitable. She was still too slow at nineteen and a half knots and the new liner the 'Oceanic' was announced as her replacement in 1928. In 1930 her passenger and crew capacity was 523 first, 841 second, 314 third class and 625 crew. In 1932 came her final Atlantic voyage, thereafter she cruised in the Mediterranean out of British ports, and in the winter operated West Indian cruises. In 1934 the *Homeric* became part of the merger between Cunard and White Star. In 1935 she was withdrawn from service and laid up off Ryde, Isle of Wight. Sold for scrap in February 1936 for £74,000 she was broken up by Thomas W. Ward at Inverkeithing before her interior furnishings were dismantled and transported by fourteen wagons to Stonehouse Railway Station.[1]

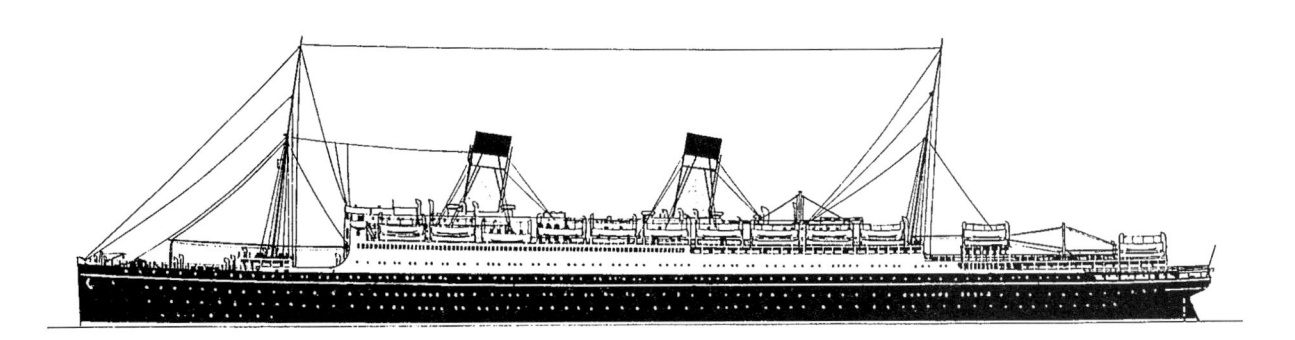

John Sheeran was a showman by trade, originally dealing in slot machines before it was outlawed. He then invested his savings in the Rex picture house, which cost £1400 to refurbish. The evolution of television, put an end to this era, and the picture house was redeveloped, returning to dealing in slot machines and amusements after the trade was legalised once more.

The picture house proved very popular especially during the war years. The first picture shown was 'It happened one night' starring Clark Gable and Claudette Colbert. At this time the seating prices were 6^D for the front stalls, 9^D for the back, 1/3^D for the front balcony and 1/- for the rear balcony.

During the war years the Rex was also used for war fund cabaret performances. Sir Harry Lauder was the chairman of this committee and was a 'regular' in entertaining audiences and wounded soldiers in the cinema. Mr Sheeran was a founder member of the committee which raised over £1700 for local soldiers. John Sheeran died in June 1967 at the age of seventy three. Many celebrities graced the Rex including Will Fyffe CBE on Sunday 21st February 1943. The Rex was the only stage on which Harry Lauder and Will Fyffe appeared together on the same bill.

Recently a cruise ship called the *Homeric* was built, and now sails from Dover round the Arctic to Scandinavia. The Rex today is used as a store for the family business, but inside it still retains many of the features and character that made it one of the most attractive picture houses in the country.

The first recording of 'moving pictures' in Stonehouse appears to be in April 1898, taken from the *Hamilton Advertiser*:

Reference: 1 White Star Line (Merchant Fleets No.19), **Passenger Liners of the World since 1893**

CINEMATOGRAPH ENTERTAINMENT

A large audience turned out on Tuesday night to witness a cinematograph exhibition in the Public Hall. A large number of views were thrown on the screen, but whether it was owing to defective films or the machine itself, a kineoptoscope. the living photographs were very indistinct, and failed to give satisfaction. Perhaps the most interesting pictures were some photographs taken by the x-rays, notably the skull of a living soldier, showing the position of bullets. The exhibition was under the management of Mr Wm. Grant, of Talgarth, South Wales, and the illuminant used was the Ethoro lime-light.

From 1896 to 1902 George Gray (The Cross) made a fine collection of glass slides depicting many scenes and characters of that time. In February 1898 there was a viewing of these slides in the Public Hall, advertised as a 'Magic Lantern Exhibition'. The glass slides have been in many hands through the years but now the Heritage Group has secured them for preservation and exhibition purposes. Unfortunately, many of the two hundred and fifty slides are either broken or damaged and apparently many have emigrated with the Gray family to America. John Melvin (Angle Street) was also a keen photographer in this era but alas few of his pictures survive in the village. He also emigrated and many of his slides went with him, others were broken up and buried in the back garden of the late George Wilson's house.

The Stanis Weavers 1750-1850

Weaving has existed in Scotland ever since the first communities were established. By the twelfth century weavers were an established part of Scottish industry. Stonehouse is thought to originate from the time of St Ninian's travels in the fourth century but prospered and developed mainly due to the weaving boom during the eighteenth and nineteenth century. It is also true that Stonehouse thrived due to its elovation from burgh to barony. This dates back to at least the year 1259, when Stanhous is mentioned at an inquest in Dumbarton.

During the period 1790-1850 Scottish hand weaving experienced great swings in the variety of fabric worked. Before 1790 the dominant linen producing weavers gradually changed to producing cotton until the mid nineteenth century .

Percentage of Scottish Hand Looms

1790	linen	72%	1826	linen	30%
	cotton	11%		cotton	60%
	silk	11%		woollen	10%
	woollen	6%			

It is presumed that by 1826 the numbers employed in silk manufacture had dwindled so low they were excluded from consideration. With the evolution of silk gauze and the shawl trade around 1840 the silk manufacturers established ten percent of all hand looms in Scotland. Silk manufacture centred mainly around Paisley but Stonehouse became predominantly a silk weaving community employing 500 by 1891. Silk weaving took considerable skill and training and more complex equipment whereas other fabrics were more easily produced with ess skill. The numbers employed in weaving in the parish steadily grew from 131 in 1792 to 400 in 1841, rising to a peak of 531 in 1861 out of a male workforce of 792.

Approximate number of Hand Loom Weavers in Scotland 1780-1880

Date	Approx. No.
1780	25,000
1800	58,000
1820	78,000
1840	84,560
1850	25,000
1860	10,000
1880	4,000

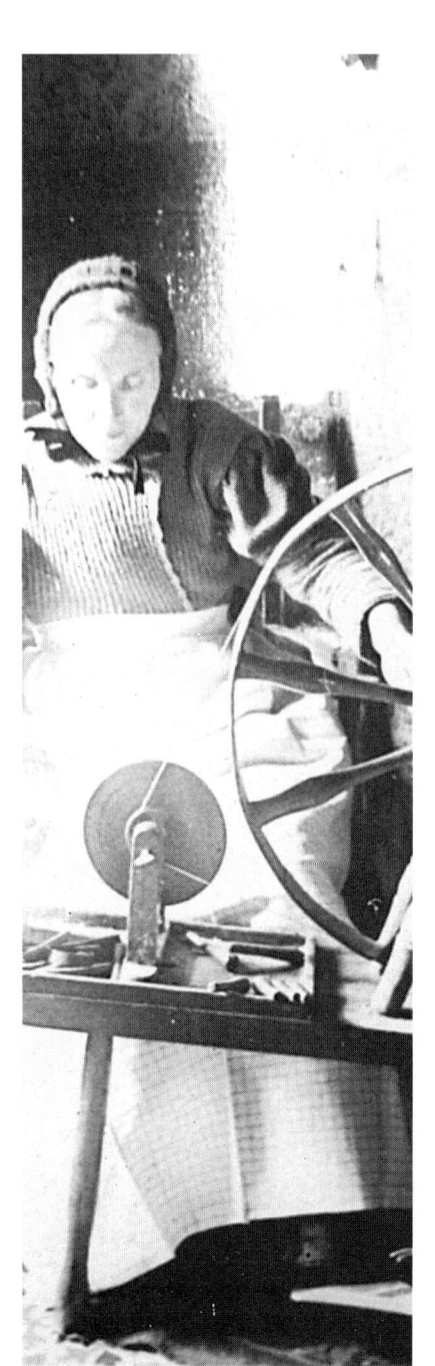

Hand loom weaving was a family business, the trade being handed down from father to son. There was a great dependency on women in the weaving process. Women were involved in pin winding, tambouring and embroidery.

The innovations of Hargreaves, Cartwright Crompton and Kay revolutionised the weaving industry around 1770, reaching its peak after the invention of the Jacquard handloom at the latter end of the nineteenth century. The Jacquard handloom changed the style of weaving dramatically by enabling the weaver to produce five intricate patterns.

The Stonehouse weavers obtained their materials from agents in the village as well as from Strathaven and Larkhall. These agents included Thomas Frew of Queen Street, Strathaven, Caldwell and Young of King Street and Robert Miller of Camnethan Street, Stonehouse, representing an English firm and several smaller agents. After several weeks the weavers returned the cloth for payment. In 1790 Rev. James Morehead reported that few weavers owned their own business, most being employed by manufacturers elsewhere. Raw cotton had been imported into Britain ever since Tudor times, but it was not until the seventeenth century that fine cottons such as muslin were imported from India. The quality of these materials, particularly muslin, were to revolutionise the weaving industry in Scotland, especially on the west coast, including Stonehouse.

Working closely with Strathaven, the Stonehouse weavers produced silk scarves, hankerchiefs and assorted exports for the Indian as well as the home market. As power loom weaving increased, the hand loom weavers could not compete with the prices of cotton, woollen and linen materials due to the materials being bought in larger quantities.

In 1841 there was talk of decline, despite the fact that there were four hundred weavers working. The power looms had taken their toll, and many could not compete. In Stonehouse the weavers were able to adapt better than others, specialising in fine silks. The industry, however, continued to suffer with fierce competition from machine made fabrics. The American Civil War was to strike another nail in the coffin of the weaving industry when it virtually stopped the import of cotton and muslin. Despite the decline, Stonehouse weavers established a reputation in the craft of silk hand weaving which continued until the demand for silk material dropped after the First World War.

Up until 1820-1830 handloom weaving was the highest paid job an ordinary working person could do. Master weavers were the best paid of the weavers and his house would be about the best sort of working class housing available at the time. As the pay became poor and work scarce, the weavers towards the end of the nineteenth century turned to work in agriculture or the mines to supplement their income. The First World War had ended the domination of the handloom as the predominant industry. Stonehouse became a mining village.

February 1879
WEAVING TRADE
Since the new year the handloom weaving has been slack. The silk fabrics are neither so plentiful nor so well paid as they formerly were. Some sorts are in little or no demand, and there seems to be nothing new to take their place. Heddled work is extremely difficult to obtain, and consequently many hands are idle in this department. A silk manufacturing firm are sending a large portion of their pirns ready wound and this is throwing the pirn winders out of employment.

In the second half of the nineteenth century there were still weavers working in Hamilton, Larkhall, Stonehouse and Strathaven. For the outlying villagers, before the days of the railway, it also meant a long walk. The last two weavers in Lanarkshire, as far as we can tell, were the Hamilton Brothers, Robert and James, of Camnethan Street. James Hamilton died at the age of eighty four in 1959 and completed his last 'wab' in 1939. The silk loom belonging to the Hamilton Brothers now rests in the Royal Scottish Museum, Edinburgh. In Rev. Robert Pollock's statistical account of 1950 he states that there were still working looms in the village but that they were principally museum pieces. When these were taken away is uncertain. Today small reminders of this once prosperous industry can still be found, such as shuttles and bobbins in the attics of weaving cottages.

Living Conditions

When weaving was at its peak in the early 1800s, the weavers were prosperous enough to own their own property. Streets of privately owned cottages were built, such as those in Hill Road and Camnethan Street. The houses were generally, though not always, one storey terraced houses with the front door opening to the street. This door led to a stone-flagged entry which gave access to the weaving shop on one side and to the living quarters of one or two rooms to the other. A ladder from the entry to the loft gave storage and extra sleeping space. A washhouse was usually added at the rear of the building. The weaving shop would hold from one to six looms which were worked by the weaver and his family. The first of these houses cost approximately £45-£60, with the repayments being only a little more than the cost of rent. The introduction of building societies around 1830 led to progressive new building developments and with the establishment of two friendly societies in the mid nineteenth century a sickness relief fund was set up for weavers. Many of these cottages have been restored, retaining the character and fine sandstone architecture.

Originally all these cottages were thatched. During the hot summers, the thatched roofs were prone to fires, which could often spread to ajoining cottages. In 1857 the nearest fire service was in Hamilton. In the event of a fire, the people would be alerted by a bell in the old jail house. Fires were quite common in the eighteenth and nineteenth centuries, so the people were extremely organised forming chains of buckets from the nearest well. In 1857 the Black Bull was burned to the ground despite the valiant efforts of the crowd. Not long before this, around 1830, the infamous Burke and Hare are said to have made a visit here, on their travels. To prevent birds nesting, a fine mesh was laid over the thatch. The last thatched cottage in the village was around the mid-nineteen sixties.

Living Room (The 'But')

The whole family had to live in this one room. As such it was actually a combined living room, kitchen and bedroom. The average family size in those days was about six to eight people, but it was not uncommon for a dozen or more to live in the one room. Many living rooms had a 'set-in' or 'hole in the wall' bed, but it was very common to have two of them side by side. At least four people would commonly sleep in these 'set-in' beds, ie, one bed; mother, father and three or four children might sleep together or with two beds—one bed might have the mother and father in it, while the other bed might contain six children. If the family was so big all could not be accommodated in the 'set-in' beds, then the surplus would sleep on straw mattresses in the loft.

Cooking

There was no gas until 1844 when a Gas Company was established to provide street lighting, neither was there electricity until around 1932-34. All cooking was done over the coal fire (coal was plentiful and cheap in Stonehouse). In Airdrie, some fireplaces may have been more 'high-tech' for the period, due to the abundance of forges and steel works nearby. In the country areas more basic fireplaces were in use.

The sort of foods consumed included porridge, vegetables, soup, oat cakes, bannocks (thick oat cakes), potatoes, buttermilk, salted herring and ling. Meat, when obtained, was generally just put in the soup. Remember there were no fridges to keep perishables, like meat, fresh. Meat had to be salted or smoked to be preserved. Bread was uncommon in Scotland in this period, wheat was not grown because of the climate—hence there was no flour to make bread. Oats being the main crop in the country, oatcakes took the place of bread in Scotland. There was a great dependence on potatoes, especially during the nineteenth century, among the poorer classes. Oatmeal, however, remained more important in the diet than bread or potatoes despite the cheapness of bread or the difficulties in preparing oatmeal. Milk, particularly in the form of buttermilk, was also popular, whereas tea, sugar, butter, salt and meat were considered luxuries. Many Stonehouse weavers used the space at the back of the cottages to grow vegetables to supplement their diet.

The weavers may have had a few chickens walking around (both in the garden and in the house) and there may have been a few eggs lying around to fry. These would have been fried in iron frying pans which many prefer today to modern pans.

Water

In the early part of the nineteenth century there was no running water supply in the cottage, (no taps, flushing toilets, baths, sinks, etc). All water supplies had to be collected from the nearest well. Going to the well for water was often a very social event. Groups of women would collect round the well to have a chat, while awaiting their turn.

Wells were common throughout the village and can be located on early ordnance survey maps. During the latter end of the nineteenth century communal taps were installed in the streets. To the best of my knowledge the first water pipes were installed in King Street, in 1894 by the County Council. It wasn't until around 1904 that water was installed into common housing.

Sanitation

Sanitation was primitive, with no sewers. It wasn't until around the turn of the twentieth century that a modernised sewerage system was built throughout the village. This system was built with the aid of the County Council through local contractors such as Robert Bruce. Many houses had dry toilets and a 'midden'. Some had a bucket or a chamber pot which was kept underneath the bed or behind the door. My parents house, still has in operation, a communal outside toilet in Townhead Street. Candermill was unique in that it had the only two-seater dry closet in the parish, which is still in evidence today. When use had been made of it, the contents were emptied on the road, as was all the household rubbish. Many houses had cesspits beside their front doors into which all the rubbish and toilet was emptied. The streets were like open sewers. If a town was fortunate it would have "scavengers", the original dustmen, who went round the streets shovelling up rubbish and taking it to the town's midden.

Because of the quantity of dung heaps and rubbish in the streets, vermin infestation (mice and rats) was common. People tried to keep their food out of the way in baskets hanging from the ceiling where the rodent had less chance of getting at it. Another effect was that the water supplies often became contaminated causing typhoid and cholera.

Washing

If the nearest water supply was over a hundred yards away, one can imagine it was unlikely that people would have a bath in their house. (To fill a bath it would have been necessary to carry ten to twenty bucketfuls of cold water). Bathing was not as fashionable in those days as it is now. If people washed at all, they generally used a jug and basin. These did not have to be copper, they were often made of stoneware or china.

As there was no water supply in the house or garden, washing the clothes had to be done in the nearest stream. There is a pool on the Avon called 'washing green hole' near Birkenshaw. The tubs (or "bines") were filled up with water from the stream. The clothes, sheets, etc, were placed in the water, then the women hitched up their skirts, stepped into the tubs in their bare feet and proceeded to tramp the clothes like treading grapes.

If they needed hot water to boil the clothes they would take the big soup pot down with them and build a fire under it. Once the clothes were washed they were laid out on the grass or over hedges to dry. Many towns and villages such as Stonehouse had communal drying greens where most of the women would go to hang up their washing. There was at one time, a place such as this at Green Street.

Soap was available if there was a candle factory nearby or if the people cared to make it themselves. Home-made soap was made by boiling animal fat for hours on end (a very smelly process) until a scum formed on top. This scum was scrapped off and became soap as it cooled down.

Washing clothes was a hard slow process, generally done every five or six weeks. Most people might have had only a couple of suits of working clothes and would wear the same clothes for two weeks. They would also have a good set of clothes for "Sunday best".

Lighting

Candles
Candles were made from tallow (made from animal fat, by a very smelly and unpleasant process). In 1836 a small establishment manufactured cotton into lamp and candle wicks. This company probably thrived in the area due to the lime extraction and mining in the parish.

Cruzie lamps
Before 1860 the cruzie lamp was the standard oil lamp. Fish oil, whale oil or oil made from animal fat was put in the top tray, along with a wick at the spout (the oil seeped up the wick). The lower tray caught any drips from the top tray as the wick was burning.

In addition to the smells of cooking, dampness, unwashed bodies and toilet waste, many houses might also have the reek of burning fish oil vapour. People too poor to have candles or cruzie lamps would collect rushes from streams. Once dried out they were placed in wooden holders and burned for light (very smoky).

Street Lighting
A gas company was established in 1844, through investment from shareholders. The company was based at the foot of Union Street, where it supplied gas to the Street Lighting Company. Although poorly lit, the street lighting was of great need in the long dark winter nights. Through improvements and further investment, the Street Lighting Company was able to install twenty seven gas lamps by 1888. This company later came under the control of the Parish Council in September 1897.

At night a lamp lighter (the 'leerie'), went along the streets lighting lamps with a long pole with a flickering flame on one end. The children were fascinated by this and the lamp lighter often found he had a crowd following him. In 1899 Robert Bruce was appointed lamplighter to the village. The production of gas proved profitable for the coal mines, for in 1883 the gas company consumed two hundred and twenty nine tons. In 1884 street lamps were supplied with gas free of charge. Gas still lit the streets until around 1950 with the exception of a few lights in the newly developed 'electric' scheme.

Religion & Politics

The Scottish hand loom weavers were devoutly religious. Not all Scottish weaving families adhered to the Established Church. The influx of trade from Ireland ensured a sizeable proportion were Roman Catholic. Boghall Street in particular was known for its Irish immigrants at this time. Religion was practised at home as well as at church and often children were taught to read through reading the Bible. This was particularly the case with the weaving community, probably the most educated of all tradesmen. Politically the weavers were traditionally radical, no more so than in the 1820 insurrection to which Strathaven namely 'Perly Wilson' was famed. Ever since the beginnings of the weaving communities the weavers have been a strong force politically. They were often able to influence laws, and in 1473 were able to forbid importation of cloth from England to boost the industry in Scotland.

Working Conditions

During working hours weavers were under constant threat of damage to their health. The atmosphere within the loom shops did not help. Floors in the working place were often earth trodden and little attention was paid to ventilation. The atmosphere was moist, and materials stored in sheds often emitted a pestilent gas. Wood inside the loom shop was often green and damp, while the air was oily and fibrous due to the nature of the work. These conditions had adverse repercussions upon the health of the workforce, especially as the working day was often twelve hours long in poorly lit cottages.

The Jacquard Handloom

When the power loom outpriced the handloom in the linen, cotton and wool trades, many weavers turned to silk, especially in Paisley and Stonehouse where it flourished for many years longer than in most towns. Silk gauze had been woven in Scotland since the eighteenth century but this new product was a coloured patterned silk, woven on the revolutionary Jacquard Loom.

The Jacquard machine was the result of nearly seventy five years work by several inventors, but it was Joseph Maire Jacquard (1752-1834), who perfected the machine. The Jacquard hand loom was a revelation in its time and was popular in France in the early nineteenth century. It was not until the middle of that century that it was adopted in Britain.

The machine was mounted on top of the loom and worked by a treadle. A series of hooks attached to the harness lifted selected threads of the warp to allow the shuttle to pass through, the selection being made by a perforated roll of card programmed by the pattern. The longitudinal threads of fabric are known as the warp, and the transverse threads as the weft.

Spinning

The oldest implement for spinning was the spindle, a very slow process. It is believed the spindle was invented in India about 2,000 years ago. The spindle was developed and incorporated on a wheel for unwinding raw silk for cocoons by the Chinese. This method was improved in India and reached Britain by the fourteenth century. The European version was initially used for wool produce and is became known as the wool wheel.

By the end of the eighteenth century, the use of spinning wheels was common, particularly the muckle wheel and the more sophisticated 'saxon' wheel which is more familiar today. The purpose of the spinning wheel was to twist the fibres being spun and wind the resulting yarn on to bobbins. The process used in spinning has remained unchanged in 2,000-3,000 years, through experimentation with the natural materials available to man. With the introduction of the wool wheel, twisting and winding still remained time consumingseparate operations, but with the development of the bobbin and flyer, twisting and winding were combined in one operation. During the eighteenth century, linen became one of the most important industry in Scotland.

Woollen thread spun at home would be sold or used for knitting or embroidery. In addition to spinning for their own needs, women could earn a little money spinning for a weaver and the wider market.

Tambouring

When Stonehouse was prosperous as a weavers' town, weaving was a predominantly male occupation. Women and girls often worked "tambouring"—a type of embroidery. Cloth was stretched over a circular frame (like a drum or tambourine) and then embroidered with flowers or whatever design was required. The women worked in their own homes and work was given out by an agent. They might have to work twelve to fifteen hours per day in order to make five to ten shillings per week.

Samplers

Many working class girls did not go to school prior to 1850. They had to work as soon as they were able. Young girls in ordinary working families did samplers in order to practise their needlework with the object of getting a job (such as embroidering flowers on tablecloths). Girls in rich families also made needlework samplers, but just as a pastime.

A common example of a sampler would include the letters of the alphabet and might also contain the names of the family in boxes (father, mother and sister, etc.) and various objects depicted in needlework. Although there was much writing on the sampler, the girl might not necessarily have been able to read or write. Often girls who made samplers were just following a pattern made up for them by someone else. Usually the ages of 'sampler' sewers ranged from five to thirteen years. Examples of samplers can be found at the John Hastie Museum, Strathaven and the Airdrie Weavers Cottage Museum.

Mining

Since the beginning of time the earth has consistently undergone change, earthquakes, floods, ice ages and droughts. Whatever the change, the earth records it. These records are there to read, if you know what to look for.

In Stonehouse if you want to know about the distant past, simply take a walk down by the banks of the Avon. Here you will find rocks and stones that tell the history of Stonehouse. Sandstone, limestone, ironstone, shale, slate, coal, even fossils. These materials became important providing work in sandstone quarries, ironstone mines, oil shale mines, lime works and collieries.

Fossils can be found in parts of the Avon Gorge, mainly of plant stems and leaves but one can also find shells. These dated from between 600 million and 800 million years old and are proof that, at one time, Stonehouse was beneath water. In the late nineteenth century, James Thomson (geologist from Glasgow), discovered a piece of carboniferous shale containing several bones of the head and teeth of 'Diplodus Gibbosus', an ancestor of the present day Stingray.[1]

The first railway lines in the village were laid to transport coal from the mines. Oil extraction from shale was developed by James 'Paraffin' Young around 1840 and was worked near the Ritchies dam on the Avon, though no remains can be seen of the site today. A large storage tank from the shale mine can still be seen in the Avon, down river towards the meetings. The shale was heated close to where it was extracted because of the huge amounts of shale needed to extract the oil. It took a ton of good quality shale to produce forty gallons of oil.

The coal mines provided most jobs after the decline of the weaving industry. Over two hundred worked at Canderrigg Colliery at its peak. This pit, also known as Broomfield, was situated just outside Stonehouse, closed in September 1958, though its remains can still be seen today. In 1842 the Government passed an Act preventing women and children working in the mines. Prior to this many children, even women would have worked many of the mines in the parish.

Records show that the numbers of miners in the parish increased from 44 in 1861 to 139 in 1871. During the late nineteenth century there was a pit known as the Garibaldi Pit near to the Spion Kop Colliery, immortalised in the line of an old poem of the time.

Are ye aye working ower at Garibaldi yet?
That's a place no' likely ever I'll forget
For I began tae work as soon as I was fit
And I started first at Garibaldi Pit.[2]

*Reference: 1 Stonehouse, Traditional and Historical. 2 Hamilton Advertiser

Despite the extensive deep mining in the parish the village has suffered no ill effects of undermining or land disfigurement, unlike opencast mining which destroys the environment and wildlife, not to mention associated health problemsl. According to local newspapers many fatalities and injuries to workers ocurred in the mines. Poor lighting, ventilation, coal dust and safety measures resulted in many dying at an early age. Explosions were commonplace and rescues proved just as dangerous. In the late nineteenth century about 800 miners were killed annually in Scotland. Innovations by Watt, Davy, Faraday and Stephenson however, helped to improve working conditions.

In 1913 Scottish coal production peaked at forty two million tons with a workforce of 148,000, thirty times greater than in 1750. When World War I took place, coal mining lost a quarter of its export trade, which it was never to regain. The fact that other energy sources were emerging, such as, hydro power, gas and petroleum, did nothing to aid the future of the coal industry. In an industry trying to cut costs, the obvious choice was to cut wages and manpower, leading to conflict in the labour force. The General Strike of 1926 was followed by a prolonged coal strike expressing the feelings in the country at the time. Mining was never to recover from this period and many people emigrated in the hope of a new and prosperous life to countries such as the U.S.A., Canada, Australia and New Zealand.

In 1924 the Miners' Welfare Institute was built for local miners, incorporating five snooker tables, a library and a reading room. With the loss of the mines in the late fifties the Institute was sold to the District Council in 1956 for public use.

A noted miner from the village was William Pearson, who despite being born in Armadale spent much of his early life in Stonehouse (Kirk Street) and working years at Canderrigg Colliery. William Pearson was elected as checkweigher at Canderrigg in 1931 and quickly became involved in the Miners' Union. In 1940 he was elected President of the Lanarkshire Miners' County Union and in 1942 he became treasurer of the NUSM and, later, General Secretary. In 1950 he was elected President of the Scottish Trade Union Congress. Another prominent Union official who today resides in our village is Andrew Clark who through the 1950s was Secretary of the Scottish Miners' Youth Committee. In 1953 Andrew was present at the miners gala day in Edinburgh, where he was a speaker to an audience of over 100,000 people.[1]

In 1947, the coal industry was nationalised by the Labour government. In that year there were 190 pits of various sizes. By 1987 there were only five working pits in Scotland producing 3.4 million tons of coal and a further 2.5 million tons from opencast coal.

The earliest record of mining in the parish is in the 1790 Statistical Account when it was noted that mining was taking place near Castlehill owned by Mr Lockhart. In 1792 there were six mines in the parish of Stonehouse

Canderrigg Colliery 1936-1939

The information below was supplied by the assistant cashier of Canderrigg, Jimmy Leggate, and gives a detailed report on the job remit of each employee and a breakdown of his wages. During this period, just before the war, the owner of the colliery was James Nimmo and Co. Ltd.

Manager
Responsible for all aspects of work at the pit, both underground and on the surface.

Under Manager
Assistant manager responsible for compiling register showing number of 'shifts' worked during the week by underground workers and amount of coal produced by each miner.

Oversman
Responsible for the supervision of all sections of the pit, especially safe working conditions.

Fireman
In charge of all men in this section, Authorised in 'shot fires' and handling of explosive materials.

Reference: 1 **A History of the Scottish Miners**

Miner
The real coal miner at the coal face. Assisted by 'drawer' who pulled loaded hutches for movement to coal bottom.

'Oncost' Worker
As the name suggests, not regarded as truly productive. Employed in various ways to assist the efficient running of the pit. e.g. laying of rails and repairs etc.

Brushers
Regarded (themselves) as the 'elite' of underground workers. Responsible for cleaning all dirt and stone from the coal face to allow the coal to be 'stripped'. Also cleaned 'left coal' which had not been won by the miner.

Machineman
There were two machinemen on each coal cutting machine at Canderrigg. These machines were either Anderson Boyes & Co. Ltd. or Mavor & Coulson Ltd., all ten inch or twelve inch machines. Some sections were about eighteen inches high.

Hole Borer
Bored holes in coal face to allow blowing down of coal. Before the advent of machine boring equipment a hatchet hand borer was used, requiring great strength.

Haulage workers
One man was in charge of a small group, responsible for maintenance and repairs of the haulage system, which conveyed coal from the pit bottom, before being 'caged' to the surface. This group was adept at rope splicing, which was a tricky operation.

The above were the main operators, although various others were employed as non producers. Their duties were as important as the others in ensuring an efficient production operation.

The wages and deductions are of great interest, as today's generation would probably find it unbelievable that a man could work in such poor conditions for pay that today would be considered a pittance. These wages were based on a six day week. The salaries of staff such as the Manager, Undermanager and Oversmen were all processed by head office.

Welfare was the contribution for the upkeep of the Miners' Institute in the various villages in the area, such as in New Street. *Ambulance* was a contribution for operating of ambulances which were unfortunately required quite often at the colliery.

Miner at coal face (6 day shifts at 8/6)			Deductions				
	Gross	**Welfare**	**Ambulance**	**Unemployment**	**Nat. Ins.**	**Total**	**Net**
Pre-Decimal	£2-11-0	4d	2d	10d	9d	2/1	£2-8-11
Decimalisation	£2.55	2p	1p	5p	5p	13p	£2.42

Oncost worker (6 day shifts at 8/-)			Deductions				
	Gross	**Welfare**	**Ambulance**	**Unemployment**	**Nat. Ins.**	**Total**	**Net**
Pre-Decimal	£2-8-0	4d	2d	10d	9d	2/1	£2-5-11
Decimalisation	£2.40	2p	1p	5p	5p	13p	£2.27

Brusher (6 back shifts at 10/6)			Deductions				
	Gross	**Welfare**	**Ambulance**	**Unemployment**	**Nat. Ins.**	**Total**	**Net**
Pre-Decimal	£3-3-0	4d	2d	10d	9d	2/1	£3-0-11
Decimalisation	£3.15	2p	1p	5p	5p	13p	£3.02

Machineman (6 night shifts at 10/6)			Deductions				
	Gross	**Welfare**	**Ambulance**	**Unemployment**	**Nat. Ins.**	**Total**	**Net**
Pre-Decimal	£3-3-0	4d	2d	10d	9d	2/1	£3-0-11
Decimalisation	£3.15	2p	1p	5p	5p	13p	£3.02

Hole Borer (6 night shifts at 9/-)			Deductions				
	Gross	**Welfare**	**Ambulance**	**Unemployment**	**Nat. Ins.**	**Total**	**Net**
Pre-Decimal	£2-14-0	4d	2d	10d	9d	2/1	£2-11-11
Decimalisation	£2.70	2p	1p	5p	5p	13p	£2.57

Haulage worker (6 day shifts at 9/6)			Deductions				
	Gross	**Welfare**	**Ambulance**	**Unemployment**	**Nat. Ins.**	**Total**	**Net**
Pre-Decimal	£2-17-0	4d	2d	10d	9d	2/1	£2-14-11
Decimalisation	£2.85	2p	1p	5p	5p	13p	£2.72

A miner at the coal face was paid 1/10 $^{3}/_{4}$ for every ton of coal dug and hauled to the surface. He could earn more than the minimum if the coal was 'big'. Brushers were paid 3/0 $^{1}/_{4}$ for left coal which day shift miners had not cleared. The brusher worked for a contractor, who had contracted with management to 'brush' a section, for so much a fathom. This was calculated each week, and the men, sometimes as many as fifteen to twenty were each paid the rate as previously shown. The contractor then retained what was left of the total which could be a rare sum in these days.

As well as being paid, employees were allowed concessionary coal which amounted to three tons of coal per year at concessionary prices i.e. 12/10 per ton and 2/6 cartage or 3/6 bagged. "Water money" was also paid to the miners if they were working in a wet section of the pit. This amounted to 6d per day if required to work in oil skins.

Working in the office, Jimmy Leggate was responsible for one of the most important 'employees' at the colliery—the 'Canary'—fed with seed and water every day.

Agriculture

In 1851, thirty percent of the male employed population worked directly in agriculture. There were more men and women, engaged in farming than in textiles and mining put together, and most rural areas had been enjoying a rising population for a century. By 1901, the population of male workers employed in farming had dropped by half to fourteen percent.

There was a corresponding decline in rural population, as both men and women were lured to the towns where many new jobs were created through industrialisation. The drudgery of the field and the dairy came to be regarded as 'unwomanly'. The drift to the towns reduced the number of farm-hands in the labour market: in consequence farmers were compelled to increase wages and provide better conditions.

Improvements in agricultural methods, changes in crop rotation and extensive drainage helped the farming industry to develop. Our farming land is predominantly clay based but was greatly enriched with the opening of the Glasgow rail link, when the contents of the Glasgow 'middens' were transported to the fields to be scattered and ploughed into the soil. In 1881 at 40 Camnethan Street there resided a man by the name of William 'Soddon', who had the appropriate occupation of field drainer.

In the early eighteenth century corn and grass were commonly grown within the parish as was flax which slowly disappeared out towards the end of the century. During the nineteenth century oats, potatoes, turnip, beans and barley were more cultivated. Hay was sold in large quantities, but wheat was not as extensive as before. In 1895 corn and hay were cut by horse drawn machines, later to be replaced by threshing machines, owned by Mr. Riddell of Lockhart Street. Travelling from farm to farm to thresh the corn, these machines were large and steam driven with a top speed of only three mph. By law a man carrying a red flag had to walk in front of the machine to warn people and horses of its approach and noise. After threshing the grain was taken to Cander Mill to be ground, coarsely or finely, according to the farmers requirements.

Cheese was produced in quantity until the mid nineteenth century, but with improvements to the railway network, milk was easier to transport and cheese was produced elsewhere.

There are approximately fifty farms in the parish now, nearly all the land is arable, and all the farms are dairy concerns.

Trades

In the nineteenth century Stonehouse was far from being just a weaving community. The village was self supporting. There were many occupational trades such as blacksmiths, millers, lime-burners, masons, carpenters, carters, joiners, grocers, drapers, publicans, shoemakers and tailors.

As a result of transport improvements many were able to sell their goods elsewhere by the ever improving road network and the introduction of the railway. Communications were also improved by the establishment of the first Post Office in 1836 aided by daily coaches to Glasgow and the coast. In 1899, John Thomson (Camnethan Street), was reported as replacing the retiring William Stevenson as postmaster. It was around 1830 the turnpike system was introduced whereby traders outwith the village had to pay a toll to sell their produce at the fairs and agricultural shows. The turnpike system was abolished around 1880. The fairs and the new rail network also attracted tourism. The Black Bull Hotel and the Royal Hotel in Trongate were popular with both holiday makers and overnight visitors. Both toll houses still stand today, the first being at Meadowside Cottage (East Bar Toll) in Lockhart Street and the other Tinto View on Strathaven Road. Under the Town Improvement Association, the first telephone office and exchange were installed at the Post Office in July 1914.

In 1836 there was a small firm manufacturing candle wicks from cotton. This company was still trading in 1950, when fire lighters were being produced. At this time a third of the workforce were miners at Canderrigg Colliery and Broomfield. By the end of the 50s many of the mining families moved to other coal fields, seeking work in Fife and Ayrshire.

Another major work place, had from the mid eighteenth century to the Great War, was Overwood Quarry. This site was formerly accessed by a small wooden bridge. Manned almost totally by local men, the quarry supplied sandstone which was used in the construction of Glasgow tenements and many important buildings including the Glasgow Herald offices (Buchanan Street), Mitchell Library (St. Andrew's Halls, Barclay Street), Sanitary Chambers (Montrose Street), Clydesdale Bank (St. Vincent Place) and the Stock Exchange in Buchanan Street.[1] A light railway was built to connect Overwood at Candermains Gully to the main line for transport to Glasgow on a daily basis. This line was also used to transport coal from the neighbouring mines such as Spion Kop Colliery. Apparently, the bridge crossing the Cander was badly engineered and by the end of World War I was dismantled for scrap. In 1893 Messrs. Baird and Stevenson of Glasgow held the lease for the quarry. It was during this period that Overwood was at its peak, constantly employing local men to keep up with demand. The site is now being used as a landfill site for waste produce. Unfortunately the facing of the sandstone from the quarry tended to scale and rot set in due to the poor quality of the stone. This ultimately led to the quarry's closure. It is notable from nineteenth century *Hamilton*

Reference: 1 **Memoirs of the Geological Survey, Scotland (Area IX)**

*Advertiser*s that there were a great number of accidents and fatalities attributed to the quarry, to which Dr. Rae was a regular visitor.

The tileworks was also a thriving business at this time. Situated at the bottom of Union Street, little is known of this company other than its popular owner of the time, John Borland. Directly across from the gasworks lay one of many clay holes, later filled in with refuse. There was also a clay hole for making the tiles on the site of the football pitch where Stonehouse Violet now play. A second brick and tileworks at Greenburn in the 1850s was owned by Dr. Mitchell, a popular employer, who would annually pay excursions for his staff to places such as Rothesay.

After the Second World War the parish rapidly became a fruit growing district with around forty five holdings growing tomatoes and strawberries. Unfortunately, competition from countries such as South Africa put an end to this industy although a few greenhouses still produce tomatoes for the home market.

George Wilson (Stonehouse) Ltd. during the 50s employed over 1000 men in the building trade, many of whom came from outwith the parish. Today the main workplace is the Stonehouse Hospital Trust, but, just as we lost the miners and the weavers, there are proposals for the closure of Stonehouse Hospital by the end of the century.

The Railway

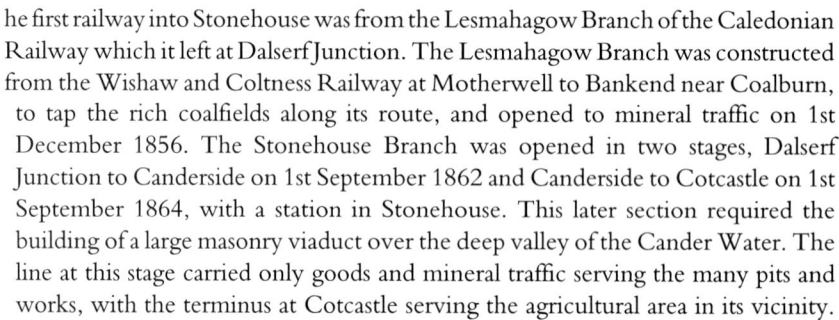

The first railway into Stonehouse was from the Lesmahagow Branch of the Caledonian Railway which it left at Dalserf Junction. The Lesmahagow Branch was constructed from the Wishaw and Coltness Railway at Motherwell to Bankend near Coalburn, to tap the rich coalfields along its route, and opened to mineral traffic on 1st December 1856. The Stonehouse Branch was opened in two stages, Dalserf Junction to Canderside on 1st September 1862 and Canderside to Cotcastle on 1st September 1864, with a station in Stonehouse. This later section required the building of a large masonry viaduct over the deep valley of the Cander Water. The line at this stage carried only goods and mineral traffic serving the many pits and works, with the terminus at Cotcastle serving the agricultural area in its vicinity.

The Lesmahagow and Stonehouse Branches were then opened to passenger traffic, with trains running to Ferniegair from 1st December 1866 and through to Motherwell and Glasgow Buchanan Street from 1st April 1868. Horse buses giving a connection from Ferniegair to Hamilton West Station for Glasgow South Side ran until 2nd October 1876, when the direct line from Ferniegair to Hamilton was opened. The Lanarkshire trains were transferred to South Side, which they used until 1879 when they were accommodated in the new Glasgow Central Station.

The station at Stonehouse was located between Lawrie Street and Vicars Road on the edge of the village. These early lines enjoyed great success. The only other railway in the area was the Hamilton and Strathaven railway opened in 1863 running via Quarter to a terminus at Flemington on the outskirts of Strathaven. However, the need for expansion became apparent and the Caledonian Railway applied to Parliament for authority to proceed. The Act was granted in 1896 and was known as the mid Lanarkshire Extension Lines Act. This allowed the Caledonian Railway to make the extensions. These were the Merryton Junction on the Lesmahagow Branch to Stonehouse; Stonehouse to Coalburn; Cotcastle to Strathaven; Strathaven to meet the Glasgow and South Western Railway line coming up from Darvel.

The line from Merryton Junction to Stonehouse required two large viaducts to be built over the valley of the River Avon. Larkhall Viaduct is a six span steel truss bridge built on the straight, on a rising gradient of one in eighty towards Stonehouse, five hundred and thirty feet long and a hundred and seventy feet high. The spans were carried on masonry piers of locally quarried stone, whose foundations sat on a bed of solid rock sixty feet below ground level. The viaduct contained 1399 tons of steel and was reputed to be the highest in Scotland. It was also subject to a speed limit of fifteen miles per hour to trains passing over it. Stonehouse Viaduct was of similar construction built in 1904. This was an eight span steel truss bridge built level on a curve a hundred and fifty eight feet above the river and contained 2273 tons of steel. Both viaducts, built by Arrol and Company of Glasgow, incorporated expansion joints on the tops of the piers to allow for the creep of the steel during hot weather. Over the years they were the scene of many suicides. Though the viaducts were built wide enough for double tracks, only single track was ever laid on them. These new single track lines were operated by the electric token block system between the crossing places. James Wyper served as Station Master before the turn of the century, retiring in 1901, after forty years service. He was replaced by David Smith and later James Rattray.

To cope with the new works, Stonehouse Station was greatly enlarged and opened in its new form on lst July 1905. At the same time as the new lines opening, the station had changed from a small platform on a branch line, to a busy junction. It now had two main platforms, a loop platform and a bay platform. This latter was used to provide a Strathaven connection. If the train was proceeding to Coalburn, the connecting train used the bay. Two signal boxes controlled traffic to the Stonehouse East and West Junctions with the station platforms between the boxes. A water column for locomotive purposes stood on the main platform. There was also a large goods yard with a stone-built goods shed, with a crane on the village side of the station and housing for key staff on the site.

A link line from the Strathaven line to the Coalburn line, allowing direct running between the two, bypassing Stonehouse Station, was constructed at this time but was never connected for some reason. A steady traffic built up with the farmers carting their milk to the station every morning. Livestock, butter, eggs and all manner of produce were also carried. In return they collected coal, fertilisers and other requirements. The local merchants and tradesmen used the station to receive and forward goods. A healthy passenger traffic built up with Sunday School trips in summer from the industrial parts of Lanarkshire to Stonehouse Park. Local schools and churches used the trains for their away days. In the 1930s there were direct evening excursions to Troon, Prestwick and Ayr costing 1/3d return. Passengers would find accommodation in the resort every evening and return from their excursion the following day. There was also a steady year round traffic with passengers travelling to and from work and people using the trains for social purposes in the evenings. In the days before the universal use of motor vehicles everything went by train and everybody travelled by train. There were also coal trains passing through at all hours, from the many collieries in the area and empty wagon trains returning to the pits. As the coal companies owned the wagons they had to go back to the owning colliery, as they alone were allowed to use them. The station became, in time, the heart of the community, and the Station Master became an important member of it.

On 1st January 1923 the Caledonian Railway become part of the London Midland and Scottish Railway. By the early thirties the motor bus and the motor lorry were making serious inroads into the traffic dealt with at the station. The milk traffic was lost when the Milk Marketing Board undertook to uplift direct from the farms by lorry. The passenger traffic suffered from bus competition. The company began to run diesel rail buses on some of the lighter loaded services with limited success. In 1935 the Stonehouse East Junction Box was closed when the service was withdrawn from the Dalserf Junction / Stonehouse section and the branch cut back to Canderside to serve the collieries in that area. In the early thirties a lady was in charge of this signal box and on its closure the Stonehouse West signal box was renamed simply 'Stonehouse'. The section from Strathaven to Darvel was next to close in 1939, but the track was left in position and was used to store wagons awaiting repair. During the war at one point there was a solid line of wagons from Strathaven to Darvel. This section was lifted after the war finished. The masonry viaduct on the Dalserf Section was no longer used and was blown up by the Canadian Army in 1942 as a training exercise.

The railways of Britain were taken over by the Government in 1948 becoming British Railways. Passenger services ended on the Lesmahagow Branch in 1951. On 4th October 1965 under the Beeching Plan, the Merryton Junction to Stonehouse; Stonehouse Strathaven; Stonehouse Coalburn lines all lost their passenger services. These lines lingered on for a few more years for mineral traffic but were closed when the pits they served worked out. Afterwards, although the rails were lifted, the bridges in the Stonehouse area were left intact, as there was a proposal that Stonehouse would become a new town and the railway would be required again, but this fell through. The Stonehouse Viaduct was blown up for scrap in 1984 yielding 2,273 tons of high quality steel scrap, without planning permission.

The station and the railway served the community well over the years and now all that remains of a once busy railway are a few ruins, cuttings and embankments. The motor vehicle has won a final ironic victory as the village has been bypassed by a new road which has followed part of the line of the old railway.

Road Links

The first recorded transport network with other towns and villages was a horse drawn coach service from Strathaven to Glasgow. The earlieat recording of a direct coach service was from the Black Bull Hotel to Glasgow every morning, driven at one time by an Alexander McNiven. There was also a regular service from Edinburgh to Ayr, which stopped for refreshments at the Buckshead Inn. By the 1880s, however, the train had replaced the coach, with five trains running daily to and from Glasgow. With the introduction of the motorcar and road improvements, a motorised transport service was soon available. The extract below recalls the event of the first motor car in the village.

> January 1897
> **MOTOR CAR**
> *Considerable excitement was occasioned on Saturday afternoon when the motor car built by Messers J & C Stirling, of Hamilton, was driven to the door of Mr C. Stirling in Vicars Road. Numerous comments were made as to the propelling power, and it is just a pity that a close examination was not allowed to be made, as the Messrs Stirling might have profited by the inventive genius of Stonehouse, which has its station about the Cross. The absence of noise and smell was very favourably noticed, and we will be proud to hear of the continued success of the enterprising firm.*

The first omnibuses in the village wree operated by John Ferrie around 1920. His charabanc (Maxwell) also doubled as a delivery lorry for fruit and veg. Mr Burns, the owner of the Black Bull Hotel, also operated a bus hire service at the time, using an 'Albion'. Around 1923 the first passenger service was established by Robert Hamilton and James Letham Watson, 'Admiral' by name. Using Lancier buses from their garage in New Street, a regular service was run from Stonehouse to Glasgow and Larkhall to Darvel via Stonehouse and Strathaven. Henry MacFarlane (84) worked as a conductor on the buses as a fourteen year old boy and remembers well many of the villagers who worked for 'Admirals', including driver Jimmy Black and conductresses Alice McInnes (Todd), Esther Kirkland and Cissy Ferguson. A popular stop on the journey was the 'fountain' at the corner of Kirk Street. This was a well, used for refreshments and collecting water. Unfortunately, due to poor road surfaces, and constant repairs to the Lanciers, the service became unreliable and was eventually run off the road in 1927 by GOC (General Omnibus Company), the forerunner of SMT (Scottish Motor Traction Corporation). Several other firms tried to operate a bus service in the village, including Baxters, Torrance, Covenanters and the Lanarkshire Bus Company. Most of these were owner driven, but none was able to make an impression in what was the survival of the fittest. With privatisation in the early 1980s came a succession of bus companies including a local firm operated today by George Whitelaw. Located at Lochpark Industrial Estate, this company has thrived for many years now, holding off fierce competition. With ever increasing traffic congestion and the environmental effects of air pollution, the only solution appears to be a better, cheaper, and more efficient public transport system, or the result may be that we shall need a bypass for our bypass.

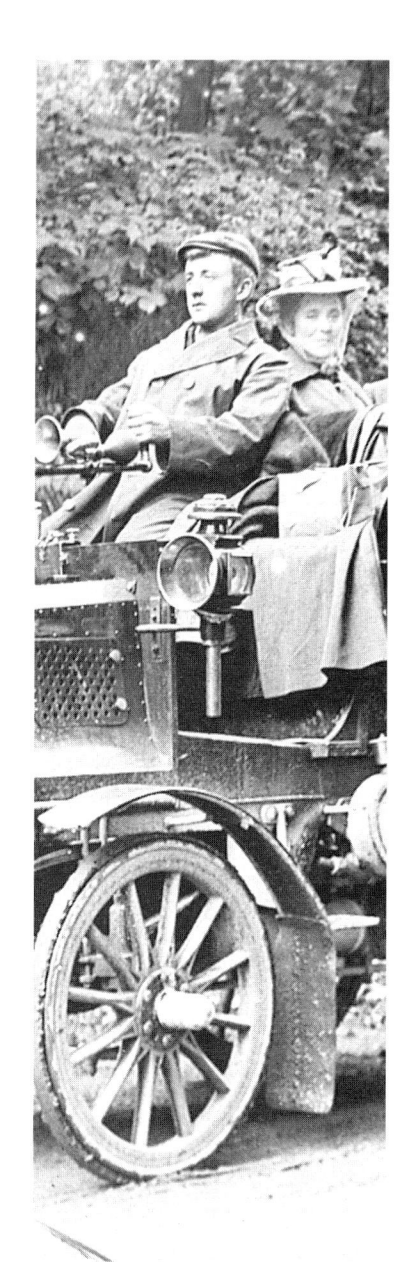

Patrick Hamilton

Patrick Hamilton was the first preacher and martyr of the Scottish Reformation. Born around 1503 he was the son of Sir Patrick Hamilton of Kinavel and Stonehouse, and nephew of the Earl of Arran. His mother, Catherine Stewart, was closely related to the royal family, being a daughter of the Duke of Albany and grand daughter of James II. As well as all his royal connections Patrick Hamilton could claim some of the most prominent and distinguished of his countrymen as his friends and relatives.

Of his early life little is known, other than he became, through family influence an Abbot of Ferne, in Rossshire, probably with a view to provide him with the necessary funds to gain an education on the Continent. In 1520 he took a degree of MA at the University of Paris. He later moved on to the University of Louvaine where he was greatly admired for his intellect, liberalism and character.

On returning to Scotland in 1523 he entered St.Andrew's University and was considered a man of great talent in learning. Entering the priesthood before the canonical age of 25, he refused to conform to many of the laws and regulations of the Church. Confiding in friends and cathedral canons, Patrick Hamilton was critical of the church and hypocrisy practised in many of its facets.

An event, however, occurred at this stage of his life which changed his relations to his ecclesiastical superiors, and made it desirable to seek asylum elsewhere. In a Parliament held at Edinburgh, in 1525, an Act was passed, under the influence of the bishops and clergy, declaring the opinions of Luther and his disciples heretical, and forbidding strangers to introduce Lutheran books into the kingdom, under pain of forfeiting their property and exposing their persons to imprisonment.

Hamilton was not a man to conceal his new convictions. Under the ever watchful eye of the church in St.Andrews he began sowing the seeds of reform. Soon the rumour of his heretical opinions reached the ears of Archbishop Beaton in 1527, who found that he was "infamed with heresy, repugnant to the faith". Having been summoned to answer this accusation, the young reformer resolved to leave Scotland for a season with three companions to Wittenberg in Germany.

While in Germany he met Tyndale (translator of the English Bible) who, with his friend and companion John Firth set about translating the *Old Testament*. Here, these three men worked together shaping their reformist views, destined for martyrdom in the knowledge that they were preparing themselves for trial and suffering on their return home.

After a passing of six months in Germany, Patrick Hamilton returned to Scotland, to resolve at whatever risk, to make known to his fellow countrymen his beliefs and convictions. On arrival many were impressed with his knowledge and teaching. It was around this time that he was to be married, but to whom it is unknown.

He found it impossible to conceal his evangelistic labours from his enemies, and soon they became known to Archbishop Beaton. Beaton sent him a message of apparently friendly character, proposing a conference at St. Andrew's to discuss matters of the church as it would appear to be in need of reform. Though suspecting the snare which had been laid for him, he felt that it was his duty to comply with the request, knowing imprisonment awaited him. The most his family could persuade him to do for his safety was to arrange that he should not go alone, but that a party of friends and kinsmen should accompany him.

Arriving in St.Andrew's around January 1528, a conference took place, with Beaton. Hamilton both in public and in confidence, then began professing his reformist views. His liberalism in his speeches, however, made it easy to procure sufficient evidence to secure his condemnation. Hamilton, however, had many influential friends, and so it was in Beaton's interest not to provoke them, but to allow Hamilton to condemn himself by his own words.

When the danger became imminent, and when Hamilton himself refused to escape, an attempt was actually made by his friends to release him. Foreseeing the trouble that lay ahead, Sir James Hamilton, his brother, and the laird of Airdrie collected a strong force, and was only prevented by a long continued storm, from reaching St. Andrews in time. Alarmed by this, and fearing a rescue, Beaton issued an order for his immediate apprehension. Drawing a cordon around the house where Hamilton lodged, the captain of the castle demanded admission; whereupon, he surrendered. Hamilton was imprisoned and charged with certain articles, regarding which he had been previously interrogated by the Primate and his Council. Hamilton, instead of disowning, defended and established them from Scripture. Hamilton proceeded with his defence concealing nothing and speaking the truth as he saw it but in so doing was accused of denying the institutions of the Church and the authority of the Pope.

Without further delay Hamilton was condemned as an obstinate heretic, deprived of all ecclesiastical dignities and offices, and delivered over to the secular power for punishment. On the afternoon of the same day, for their business was such as required haste, he was hurried to the place of execution in front of the Old College, where a fire had been already prepared.

Taking off his cloak and giving it to a servant, Hamilton said,

> *This stuff will not help me in the fire, yet will do thee some good. I have no more to leave thee but the example of my death, which I pray thee to keep in mind; for albeit the same be bitter and painful in man's judgement, yet it is the entrance to ever lasting life, which none can inherit who deny Christ before this wicked generation.*

Having thus spoken he commended his spirit into the hands of God and being bound to the stake was burned to death. Thus died this noble martyr, on the last day of February, 1527, in the twenty fourth year of his age. "The flames in which he expired were in the course of one generation to enlighten all Scotland."[1]

Reference: 1 **Stonehouse, Traditional and Historical**

James Hamilton

Scotland's forgotten hero

The founder of this family was a descendant from the Raploch branch of the Hamilton family. James Hamilton was the eldest son of James Hamilton of Raploch and was to be the first of the branch of the Stonehouse Hamiltons. When he later married Margaret, daughter and sole heiress of Alexander Mowat of Stonehouse he acquired a considerable portion of the barony of Stonehouse by his wife.

During the reign of Henry VIII of England, Henry tried to reduce Scotland to a mere dependency of England by sending the Earl of Hertford, with Admiral Viscount Lisle, up the Firth of Forth with a fleet of two hunderd ships, besides smaller craft, and an army of 20,000 men to crush the Scots in 1544. When the news of this formidable force reached the ears of the Scottish nobles they were terror stricken and fled for their own safety. Hertford disembarked his troops and artillery, occupying four days, and it was only when the English army was on its way to Leith, that the Earl of Arran, Huntly and Argyle raised a few troops, and an attempt was made to prevent their passage further. Unfortunately, they were repulsed and made haste their retreat to Linlithgow. The English entered Leith without further opposition, and the town was given to the army to plunder.

The inhabitants of Edinburgh attempted to resist the invading foe, barricading the gates, as Hertford was coming with intent to burn and destroy. He stated that the one and only condition on which he would withdraw his army was if they would deliver up their young queen (Mary of Scotland). Henry VIII wished to gain supremacy of Scotland by arranging a marriage between Mary and his son Edward, but this was not the wish of the Scots.

This demand of Hertford's was sternly refused. The citizens prepared to resist and were deserted by their provost. Notwithstanding this, the inhabitants made a desperate resistance, keeping Hertford at bay until the heavy artillery was brought from Leith. As night came, further resistance was hopeless, and the citizens carried off as much as they could abandoning their city. When Hertford returned next day he found an Edinburgh deserted, except for the garrison, held by Captain Hamilton, Laird of Stonehouse, a gentleman of great military skill and renown, and one of Scotland's staunchest patriots.

The enemy overwhelmed the city, and there laid siege to the castle; but, under their heavy artillery, Hamilton displayed such heroic skill and valour in defence of the garrison that the English found it impossible to capture the fortress. They constructed batteries and availed themselves of all the engineering skill at their command, but dauntless Hamilton kept up an incessant and harassing fire. This was directed with precision at some of the principal officers of the besiegers, compelling them to end the siege. The English, in baffled rage and disappointment, set about the destruction of the defenceless city. Edinburgh was said to have burned for three days. As the retreating English army proceeded slowly along the coast they destroyed all that stood in their path.

If it be one of the characteristics of a true hero, to be cool and calm, to be brave and lion-hearted in a time of danger, Hamilton was a hero worthy of the best days of Scotland. By his military skill and prowess, his heroic bravery, invincible courage, and patriotic valour, our country was delivered from the invading foe, and the castle rescued from the tyrant's grasp. Though history has not acknowledged his name to paper or song by his heroic deeds he deserves a place among the brave defenders of our country in the days of yore, of Wallace, Bruce and Douglas. No monument records the valorous deeds of this illustrious Stonehousian, but the world has not lost his name, and a grateful country ought to feel proud of his imperishable renown.[1]

Hamilton was made governor of Edinburgh Castle after the invasion, and as testimony of his valour in its defence, the citizens elected him provost of Edinburgh.

> *Brave Hamilton of Stonehouse,*
> *Stern captain of the fort,*
> *Against the English army*
> *Defended every port.*
>
> *Right gallantly he held his ground,*
> *Hemmed in on every side,*
> *And poured destruction on the foe*
> *In a red streaming tide;*
>
> *Till the victor saw the vanquished*
> *Retreat, in proud disdain,*
> *Wreaking vengeance on the innocent,*
> *And plundering the slain.*[1]

Reference: 1 **Stonehouse, Traditional and Historical**

Gavin Jack

Gavin Jack went to America from Stonehouse in the year 1855 according to the 1900 US Census records. Born on 19th June 1827, the second of eight children, born to Stark Jack and his wife, Catherine McClelland, and named after his grandfather who was a barber by trade. The family stayed at 19 King Street and by the age of ten or eleven, all the children including Gavin were working with their parents in the weaving shop. According to the 1841 census he was employed as a handloom weaver by the age of fourteen. What attracted him to America we do not know but it may have been due to the declining weaving industry and the rapidly growing steel industry in America. It was here he was to find work in the steel mills of Youngstown from 1855 until the Civil War broke out, and thereafter until about 1900 when he was seventy three.

Family legend tells that Gavin Jack enlisted in the Union Army during the Civil War three times. He fought for three years and served in the seventh Regiment, Ohio Infantry, under General George Brinton McClelland and in the army of the Potomac as a foot soldier for sixteen months. His regiment was reduced to less than three hundred of the original thousand recruits as a result of death, disease and capture. Gavin later transferred into the 6th US Cavalry and fought as a cavalryman for the last twenty months of his service, until captured at Gettysburg, Pennsylvania in July 1863 by the Confederate forces and held prisoner for about two months before being exchanged.

His Civil War records describe him in 1861 as: five feet six inches, complexion—dark, eyes—grey, hair—brown and occupation—pudler (steel mill job). He was discharged from the Union Army in 1864 and married Roseanah Swauger and then lived in Youngstown until his death in 1921 at the age of 94. Gavin Jack came from a long line of Jack's in Stonehouse dating to at least the seventeenth century.

Robert Naismith

Robert Naismith, draper and historian, was born in Stonehouse on 31st August 1832, the eldest child of James Naismith (born 28.8.1796, Glassford) and Margaret Scott (married 4.11.1831). His forebears came from Jackton near East Kilbride. He married Bethia Browning Paterson at East Kilbride on 17th August 1864, and they resided at Crossview at the corner of King Street.

He took an active part in the affairs of Stonehouse but will be remembered most, perhaps, for his *Stonehouse: Historical* and *Traditional* published in 1885 where he propounded for the first time the theory of the origin of the name of Stonehouse. He also traced the proprietors of the Barony from the earliest period down to the time of his writing. As an historian he was responsible for several publications including:

The story of Christianity in Scotland	
The story of our English Bible	
The story of the Kirk	1865
Stonehouse: Historical and Traditional	1885
Robert and James Haldane: Two worthy workers of bygone days	1893
Rev. James Hamilton D.D.: A Memoir	1895
The merchant martyr of Stonehouse (booklet)	

His interest in loca and religious hsitory, were researched and documented, throwing some light on the characteristic features of a bygone age. He was an extremely active member of the community, being involved in many local organisations and county committees. In April 1878, the Heritable Investment Bank (Ltd) opened under his management.

Throughout the latter half of the nineteenth century, Robert Naismith lectured to various organisations, on his extensive knowledge of the church, the village and its history. He also built the house of Westlea, Vicars Road, where he died at 4.00pm, on Thursday 3rd March 1898.

His son Robert Johnstone Naismith, also a draper at Crossview, Stonehouse was Chairman of the School Board when the new infant department at Townhead School was opened in 1912 and his son Robert Naismith, born at Crossview, became a famous radio scientist. He was a pioneer and inventor of automatic equipment for ionospheric measurements and a member of Sir Robert Watson-Watt's team in radar research before and during the war, also the author of a number of scientific publications. His death in 1973 marked the end of this branch of the Naismith.

Archibald Mathies

On February 13th 1987 the United States Airforce training school in Upwood, Cambridgeshire was renamed the Mathies NCO Academy in honour of one of only a handful of NCOs to have been awarded the Congressional Medal of Honour, the U.S.A's highest military award. The academy had a choice of five but the choice of Staff Sergeant Archibald Mathies was an easy one.

Mathies was born in Stonehouse on June 3rd 1918, but moved to Pennsylvannia with his parents to start a new life in America. His Medal of Honour, one of only seventeen to be awarded to personnel of the 8th Air Force during World War II, was posthumous. Archie died struggling to land a B-17 in a field south of Stilton (near Cambridge) on February 20th 1944. He was buried with full honours at the US cemetery at Madinglay, west of Cambridge. His body was exhumed in 1947 and taken home to Pennsylvannia.

The citation of Staff Sergeant Archibald Mathies reads:

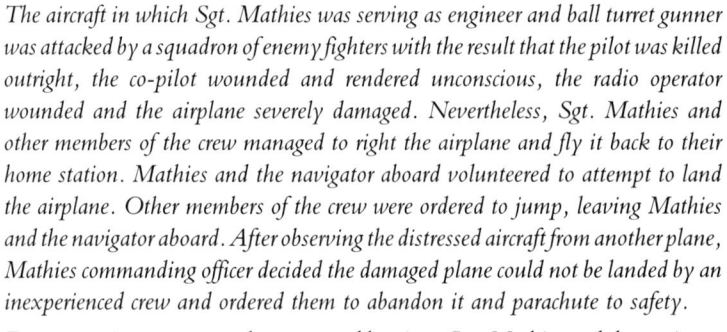

> *The aircraft in which Sgt. Mathies was serving as engineer and ball turret gunner was attacked by a squadron of enemy fighters with the result that the pilot was killed outright, the co-pilot wounded and rendered unconscious, the radio operator wounded and the airplane severely damaged. Nevertheless, Sgt. Mathies and other members of the crew managed to right the airplane and fly it back to their home station. Mathies and the navigator aboard volunteered to attempt to land the airplane. Other members of the crew were ordered to jump, leaving Mathies and the navigator aboard. After observing the distressed aircraft from another plane, Mathies commanding officer decided the damaged plane could not be landed by an inexperienced crew and ordered them to abandon it and parachute to safety.*
>
> *Demonstrating unsurpassed courage and heroism, Sgt. Mathies and the navigator replied that the pilot was still alive but could not be moved and that they would not desert him. They were then told to attempt a landing. After two unsuccessful efforts the airplane crashed into an open field in a third attempt to land. Sgt. Mathies, the navigator and the wounded pilot were killed.*

'Archie' Mathies had only joined the 351st, thirty three days earlier and was on only his second mission. The B-17 was one of over 400 B-17s on mission 226 despatched to Leipzig, targeting a Messerschmitt factory and other locations, when they were hit by a 109 over Germany. Mathies had only a couple of hours flying experience but was prepared to make the ultimate sacrifice to save the wounded pilot.[1]

Reference: 1 FlyPast

The Covenanters

During the reign of James VI the church was becoming more and more under the influence and control of the sovereign. When he ascended the English throne he tried to introduce the system of governing the church by bishops. This caused mistrust of the government which continued under the reign of Charles I who condemned private prayer meetings and conventicles in Scotland. A deep discontent festered in the hearts of Scotsmen, true to the religious beliefs of the Scottish church They refused to be pressurised by the government and rebelled. A large gathering of them assembled in Edinburgh to vindicate the cause of liberty and religion. All classes were represented, and in the spring of 1638 at Greyfriars they subscribed in supporting the National Covenant, and almost the whole nation followed in demonstrating on behalf of civil rights and religious freedom. This document circulated throughout every parish and was subscribed to with enthusiasm. A few years afterwards the differences were settled between the Scottish Parliament and the English Commissioners and Charles I paid the penalty for this and other injustices, with the loss of his head.

During the protectorate of Cromwell the country enjoyed a great deal of spiritual freedom, legitimising protestantism. This freedom was short lived when Charles II came to the throne to restore religious discontent to Scotland. He strove to bring the Church under his control and was more oppressive than his predecessors. Hundreds of followers of the Covenant were sent to the gallows as Scotland was subjected to his tyranny, as were many ministers. All those who refused to submit to the will of Charles were either imprisoned or evicted from their parishes. Nearly four hundred did not and thus began the bloody inquisition of Scotland. Ten thousand troops were let loose upon the country to execute and kill, without mercy, every armed Covenanter.

'Bloody' Graham of Claverhouse led the onslaught, but suffered defeat at the Battle of Drumclog in 1679. It is thought that Graham of Clavers (Bonnie Dundee) may have used Patrickholm House as his headquarters during the persecution of the Covenanters locally, for its occupants the Hamiltons of Raploch, were at that time fiercely opposed to the Covenanters. The proprietor of Patrickholm, William Hamilton, was extremely unpopular for his severity towards the Covenanters. Surprisingly, his two sisters were both married to prominent Covenanters. It must be remembered, however, that not everyone supported the Covenanters and their cause, especially in the Highlands. Although many regarded Graham of Clavers' as a villain, during the struggle for religious freedom, he was the toast of many during the early years of the Jacobite risings. He was killed at Killiecrankie in 1689 despite winning the battle.

John Morton was the only Covenanter lost on the field of battle. Five others died afterwards from their wounds, including James Thomson from Stonehouse. Gravestones mark the spots in the different churchyards where their remains rest. In June 1880, on the two hundred and first anniversary of the Battle of Drumclog around 2,000 people gathered for a service in St. Ninian's churchyard, to commemorate the event.

On an old map of the parish, crossed swords are found at Sodom Hill indicating a battle site. The battle may have been a skirmish between the Covenanters and 'Clavers'. The only record found of this battle taking place is from Robert K. Chalmers song 'In praise of the Avon', in the lines:

> Sodom Hill and Drumclog Field
> Where weavers fought and wadna yield;
> Where Scotland's richts were firmly seal'd
> Beside the winding Avon

It was the Battle of Bothwell Bridge only three weeks later, that sealed the fate of the Covenanters. Persecuted and hunted for their faith, their monuments stand as a silent reminder of their oppression.

James Thomson

James Thomson was a farmer from Tanhill on the west side of Lesmahagow Parish, bordering Stonehouse Parish from which his family is said to have departed around 1780, having been tenants there for near 350 years. Little is known of this martyr, except that he died from wounds inflicted at the Battle of Drumclog in 1679. He was later interred in St.Ninian's churchyard where his tomb reads:

> Here lays or near this Ja Thomson
> Who was shot in a Rencounter at
> Drumclog, June 1st 1679
> By Bloody Graham of Clavers House
> for his adherence to the
> Word of God and Scotland's
> Covenanted Work of Reformation - Rev xii 11

On the other side:

> This hero brave who doth lye here
> In truth's defence did he appear,
> And to Christ's cause he firmly stood
> Until he seal'd it with his blood.
> With Sword in hand upon the field
> He lost his life, yet did not yield.
> His days did End in Great Renown,
> And he obtained the Martyrs Crown.

His descendants renewed his stone in 1832. Both monuments are still to be seen today, with the latter taking the form of a table stone monument. In 1955 the original stone was repaired due to damage caused by the elements of nature. James Thomson's wife along with his son John, who was also a farmer, were captured and imprisoned at Blackness Castle, four miles from South Queensferry. Their fate is unknown.

The family of the martyr was in earlier times located in a place called Cunningair or Collingair in the parish of Stonehouse, opposite Dovesdale. It was from here that James Thomson's family was to travel to the lands at Tanhill. His descendents have been numerous, many of them have been ruling elders in the Church of Scotland. Many inhabitants of the village today can trace their origins from this family line. His gravestone in St. Ninian's churchyard stands as a solitary reminder of part of the village's historical past, a man who stood for a valiant cause in which so many sacrificed their lives.

Margaret Law

Margaret Law was the maiden name of Mrs John Nisbet of Hardhill. She came from the Parish of Loudon near Drumclog, and was to prove herself a true heroine of the Covenant defending her husband's beliefs to the last.

John Nisbet and his wife lived quietly and happily together until the year 1661. It was then that John Nisbet made his stance clear after the burning of the Covenant. After its renewal in 1666, John Nisbet was threatened with his life, and thus was forced to keep himself armed and vigilant at all times. At the Battle of Pentland he received seventeen wounds, was stripped naked and left for dead on the field, but was able to gather enough strength to make his escape. He took a year to recover from his wounds before playing his part in the triumphant victory at Drumclog. This success was short lived, for on the morning of June 21st 1679 the Covenanters were to be defeated at the Battle of Bothwell Bridge.

John Nisbet led a troop of Covenanters on that day but despite the bravery of these men the day was disastrous and they found themselves being hounded and hunted to their deaths. A reward of 3,000 merks was offered for the capture of Nisbet, and punishment was dealt out for those who sought to protect and shelter him.

Constantly on the run and suffering great hardships Margaret Law was resilient throughout, keeping the family together, whilst comforting and encouraging her husband during his support to the cause of free religious belief. It was during this time in hiding Margaret brought her family to Stonehouse near to the lands of Hazeldean. She is said to have dwelt in a cot house, where due to starvation, ill health and persecution she died at the beginning of December 1683. John Nisbet returned from hiding to find both his wife and daughter dead from ill health. Grief stricken he carried his daughter all the way to Stonehouse churchyard and buried her beside her mother. The minister at the time, possibly John Oliphant, refused to allow the burial of his family in the cemetery, but after being threatened by a mob in support of John Nisbet the minister was forced to let the burial go ahead.

John Nisbet was later captured while at a prayer meeting in Fenwick, taken to Edinburgh, tried, condemned, and executed at the Grassmarket on December 4th 1685.

James Hamilton of Kittiemuir

One of the earliest defenders of the Covenant was James Hamilton of Kittiemuir. He was captured at the Battle of Pentland, with those inscribed on the monument and along with ten others, they were executed on the same platform in Edinburgh, on December 7th 1666. Their heads and right arms were struck off, and displayed throughout the country as a warning to others of the same sympathies. Their heads now rest in Cadzow Street graveyard in Hamilton along with John Parker and Christopher Strang. James Hamilton is said to have been a prominent yeoman (a gentleman serving in a royal or noble household), for in public records he is said to have been mounted and armed with a sword and pistols. He, along with Gavin Hamilton of Mauldsie Mains (possibly his brother), who suffered with him, were members of Maclellan of Bascobe's troops, and appear to have joined the rebels when the Covenant was sworn. In J.H. Thomson's, *The Martyr Graves of Scotland* James Hamilton is said to have been a tenant at Killiemuir, but this is inaccurate, probably caused by the researcher not noting the t's being crossed thus "Killie" instead of "Kittie". This theory can be backed up by Robert Naismith's book 'Stonehouse Historical and Traditional' and parochial records.

John Boyd

John Boyd lived in the parish of Stonehouse and died at Craigbank in the parish of Dalserf, February 2nd 1718. John Boyd seems to have been well versed in the scriptures and well able to defend the beliefs of the Covenant. Due to his convictions, he, along with his family, were forced to flee their home to Ireland, where he was to bury six of his children and his wife before returning with his only son. He suffered great hardship during the persecution of the Covenanters but was able to elude capture until his death in Dalserf. In researching the 1696 parochial record Boyds are to be found at Burnfoot but it is not possible to ascertain if this is a direct line or not.

James Robertson of Hazeldean

James Robertson was a travelling merchant who is said to have lived mainly in the area of Hazeldean. Details of his life are scarce but what is clear is his strong adherence to his faith and the principles of the Covenant. He was well educated and possessed considerable literary talents. In 1680 he is reported to have affixed a paper, in defence of the Covenant, to the door of the old parish kirk, so well written and with such passion and conviction, that he was soon to make many enemies.

In Kilmarnock, October 1682, he went to see a prisoner of his acquaintence, John Finlay, when without provocation, he was seized and held captive for ten or twelve days. While in prison he was interrogated, mistreated, then taken to Edinburgh and further examined by the Committee of Public Affairs. Despite his strong religious beliefs and well versed testimony he could not say enough to save himself from the charge of treason. He was executed, along with William Cochrane and John Finlay, from Kilmarnock, on December 15th 1682 in the GrassMarket, Edinburgh. When he attempted to speak upon the scaffold the drums beat, and drowned his words; and when he complained, the town major beat him.

Others to have been persecuted

After the Battle of Bothwell Bridge the Covenanters were persecuted and hounded to their deaths. Many who supported the government became informers and were rewarded for their information. Sympathisers and friends of the Covenanters suffered at the hands of the government troops. Some were imprisoned and others evicted from their homes, many to perish in the cold winters of the countryside. Robert Findlay, from this parish, along with a number of others from the villages of Glassford and Avondale, were murdered in cold blood on the road near Hamilton by the king's soldiers after the Battle of Bothwell Bridge. They were on their way to hear a sermon in the camp when they were murdered. The following is a list of persons cited in the Parish of Stonehouse in May of 1683 as being Covenanters or connected with them:

James Stobo in Kittiemuir (Several Stobo(we)'s were present at Kittiemuir in the 1696 parochial records); John Hamilton in Milneholm; John Gillies; Thomas Weir in Crumhaugh (in 1696 this family can be traced to Laigh Crumhaugh); John Hamilton in Brigholm (family still present here in 1696); James Reid in Tweedie-mylne; James Wilson in Sandford; Archibald Fleming; James Miller, Boig; (this family can be traced to the area until 1841); Hans Miller in Dykehead (present in 1696 records); Thomas and James Scott in Hisledane (several Scot(t)'s can be traced within 1696 records); Thomas Miller in Stainhous; Thomas Hamilton; John Hamilton in Lenloch; James Hamilton; James Kinnock (beddell the Clerk to the session waiting); James Mutter in Stanehouse and Gavin Wood of Corslett (family can be traced to 1696 records).

In the fugitive roll for 1679 two names appear as belonging to Stonehouse: Alexander Hamilton of Langrigg (Alexanders family can be traced to both the 1696 and 1841 census), and Thomas Doicks in the village of Stonehouse.

On 26th June 1679, William Richardson of Stonehouse and others were charged with treason for joining the rebels the previous year. They appear to have been held in the Tolbooth, Edinburgh, but no record has been found of Richardson's execution.

On December 19th 1683, John Douglas of Stonehouse, along with others, was held prisoner in Edinburgh. The name of John Walker of Stonehouse appears in a fugitive list on May 5th 1684.

On 26th July 1685, John Hamilton of Millholm, was imprisoned in Dunottar Castle, but after taking an oath of allegiance, was liberated under a bond of 5000 merks (Family is still present here in 1696).

In the month of January 1686, a party of soldiers searching the country for Covenanters, came to Stonehouse and carried away eight men and two women prisoners for allegedly listening to an outlawed minister.

The Church after the reformation

After the establishment of the reformed religion in 1560, Scotland was divided into five districts, over which superintendents were placed to look after the spiritual interests of the people. A number of parishes were combined and placed under the charge of a minister, and then probationer style readers were appointed to each parish to read common prayers and scriptures until such times as a suitable minister could be found. The first reader in the Parish of Stonehouse was William Hamilton in 1560.

Today Stonehouse is still affected by the conditions set by past proprietors. A probationary clause in the sale of land agreement forbid the erection of religious dwellings other than Protestant places of worship. This agreement I believe was for the term of 999 years. A previous Duke of Hamilton when releasing his grounds, made a condition that no chapel be erected on his land (as was the condition of most Templar land).

Parish Church

Despite the industrial revolution, the ever changing environment and men's lust for war, Stonehouse has retained its character and much of its architecture. This can be seen in the Old Parish Church built around 1772, once seating nine hundred and now a wholesale 'cash and carry' owned by Ginestri's. In John Morehead's *Statistical Account of Stonehouse* in 1790 he states, "the church was re-built in 1772". Whether he meant there was a church previously on the site or built to replace the decaying Old St.Ninian's Church at the glebe is uncertain.

The first recording of anyone connected with the church was Sir Rodger, the rector in the year 1297, the same year Wallace defeated the English at Stirling bridge.

The parish kirk bell was was gifted to Rev. George R. Robertson, (minister of Hamilton Memorial Church, Stonehouse 1919-1930) by Mrs Sophia MacLeod of Galloway & McLeod Ltd and taken to Lochee Road Church, Dundee where Mr Robertson was minister in 1943. When the church building in Dundee was demolished in 1990, an arrangement was made to have the bell returned to St. Ninian's, Stonehouse. Unfortunately, the ancient relic was stolen from the site and the bell's fate is unknown. The church bell and its clock were formerly situated in the old jail house in 12/14 Lawrie Street during the eighteenth century. The county jail was later relocated to Kirk Street at the end of the nineteenth century. During the 1870s, the village had its own town crier and bellman, Peter Gray.

The church manse was built in 1761 and received improvements in the year 1816.

It was not until 1894 that it was decided that a new church was needed due mainly to a lack of space. On Saturday 18th December 1897 the new church was opened. It was not until 1929 after the Union of the Churches that the church was renamed as we know it today "St Ninian's Parish Church". The memorial stone was laid on the 17th October 1896 when a large crowd turned out to witness the ceremony. Under the memorial stone a bottle was placed containing The Scotsman, Glasgow Herald, *Hamilton Advertiser*, British Weekly, Mission Record of the Church of Scotland, Life and Work, the magazine of the Church of Scotland, Year book of the Church of Scotland, the coins of the realm, from a sovereign to a farthing and three church communion tokens dating to 1736, 1752 and 1835. There were many local dignatories at the celebrations including invited speakers, one of whom was the unfortunately named Rev. Pagan. The church was built using sandstone from the quarry at Overwood.

Free Church

The formation of the Free Church, under the title of "The Stonehouse Free Presbyterian Church Association" took place on 28th March 1843. Nearly a century later in Septemeber 1946, the Free Church joined the Church of Scotland. The first Free Church was built in December 1843 and the first minister was the Rev. W. K. Hamilton. This church cost £480 and gave thirty years service until 4th October 1874, when a new church with a 117 foot Gothic spire, was opened seating 640. Mr Baldie was the architect. Due to the amalgamation of the Hamilton Memorial Church (which had been in use for seventy two years) and St. Ninian's there was found to be no need for two churches and thus demolition work began in the year 1954.

A new congregation was formed, when it separated from the Free Church in 1893. This new congregation was admitted into the Congregational Union of Scotland in April 1894, holding its services for a time in the Public Hall. Rev. Peter Smith was ordained as pastor in the same year, but it was not until June 1896, that the present Congregational Church in Angle Street was opened, seating four hundred and fifty.

United Presbyterian Church

The first church erected in the village for the Associates Secession or Burgher denomination was built in 1796 and was roofed with the woodwork from the old Chapelton church which was dismantled and rebuilt in the village seating three hundred and sixty when completed. The first minister of the congregation was Rev. William Taylor 1798-1817. After undergoing several alterations it was taken down in 1878 in order that the present structure be erected. The new church was opened on 29th April 1879. Originally called the United Free Church it was designed to seat over six hundred people and like St. Ninian's, both churches were originally designed to have a spire incorporated. In November 1880 the church had a clock installed at a cost of £132, £30 of which was donated by an ex-resident of the village living in London. Ordained in 1842, Rev. H. A. Paterson was minister of the United Free Church until his death in 1901. The church was then renamed in his honour as Paterson Church. In 1929 the congregation refused to enter into the Union of Churches and remained the United Free Church. On January 2nd 1977 the roof and much of the interior of the church were detroyed by fire. By March the following year, however, the church was restored to its former glory.

There was a Salvation Army Hall in Kirk Street which, during the '50s, housed twenty three soldiers. The present Salvation Army Hall is situated at the top of Wellbrae. On September 1st 1904 a large crowd congregated at the Cross to welcome the founder of the Salvation Army, General William Booth, as he travelled the country campaigning.

There is no Roman Catholic Church in the parish and those who do attend chapel either travel to Strathaven or to the chapel hall in Wellbrae which was formerly the gospel hall for the Plymouth Brethren. This building was at one time the Parish Chambers. To one side of the building was the registrar of births, deaths and marriages and to the other was Mr Alexander Anderson, clerk responsible for allocating money to the poor and destitute. Not far from the Parish Chambers lay a row of weavers' cottages in what was called Parkhall, where the present Canderavon Home is now situated. Here a one metre high milestone once stood with the information, Edinburgh 38 miles and Ayr 33 miles.

Education

At least until the nineteenth century, the major impetus behind the development of education in Scotland was provided by the Church. The aim of education was primarily one of training those who would be participating in church services.

The establishment of Christianity in Scotland dates from the arrival of St. Ninian in the fourth century. The history of the early Church shows the growth of formal education taking place after the landing of St. Columba in Iona in AD 563. The Celtic and Roman churches founded schools as an extension of their work and worship. The Reformers also saw the importance of education both in its own right, and as a means of strengthening Protestantism. Even into the nineteenth century, the parish schools were controlled by the Church of Scotland. Throughout the period, therefore, learning depended much on the vision of the Church. The aim of education was primarily one of training those who would be participating in church services.

During the Reformation many Scottish schools were destroyed. The Reformer's vision was the establishment of a school in each parish which would be accessible to all children alike, whether rich or poor, male or female. Robert Owen was among those who regarded education as much as a right for working class children, as for their middle and upper class contemporaries, and pioneered a gradual change in attitude.

Most children began their schooling at the age of five. The normal leaving age, however, varied considerably, from as low as nine in Libberton and Crawford, to as high as fifteen in other parishes. Corporal punishment, using the tawse, was common throughout Lanarkshire: indeed schoolmasters maintaining discipline in this way seem to have been respected.

Throughout the years since 1872, educational provision in Lanarkshire, as in Scotland as a whole, has been expanded to meet an increasing range of needs. The first stage involved ensuring that as many children as possible who were of school age in terms of the 1872 Act actually attended school. The second stage of education provision involved organising an effective system of secondary education.

As the standards of provision have improved, so public expectations of the education service have increased throughout the century. The upheaval of two World Wars and the social deprivation between the wars created in people a desire for change. Significant Education Acts were passed in 1918 and 1945/46 and the prevailing philosophy of the 1960s also fostered innovation.

The earliest record of a school in the parish dates to around the beginning of the eighteenth century, From the parochial records we note that on May 13th 1701 a Mr Richard Steil was recommended by the presbytery of Hamilton to take the post of school master in Stonehouse.

There being no objections from the church, he took the post. On November 3rd 1702 the church session met to discuss; "That there should be three schools in the parish, one in Kittiemuir, the teacher of which is to have forty merks of the sellary allowed him; another at Tweedyside, the teacher of which is to have twenty merks of the sellary; and the principal school to continue in the town of Stonehouse, as before". Richard Steil is said to have "quit" the school at this meeting to make way for William Walker of Stonehouse as schoolmaster. Whereabouts this school stood is uncertain but the earliest clue to its siting is again from the parochial records which in May 1708 state; "The school was being held in the kirk till a fit place could be had. The committee appear to have latterly got a schoolhouse from Thomas Cure". In 1716 the schoolhouse is said to have been in a state of "ill condition" and needed to be thatched. William Walker resigned as schoolmaster in this year to be replaced by Walter Weir.[1]

In 1780 there existed a school very near to where the present Townhead Street School is situated. From the Statistical Account we are told that the school masters' house was at 44 King Street with the school a little further up the street. The school and school masters' house are said to have cost £40 to build, paid by the parish. The school house is said to have been low roofed, ill ventilated, and earth paved but reasonably well attended. The working conditions, however, did nothing to improve the health of the children. This may have been the first school built in the parish, as it appears prior to this educational establishments were merely rented. Records further state, besides the parochial school, there were others at the head and sometimes the foot of the parish. These were probably temporary dwellings rented due to a lack of permanent premises.

Reference: 1 **Parochial records**

In 1790 the parochial school master was paid the sum of three pence per quarter, by forty seven contributors, though this money apparently was often difficult to collect. According to the minister at the time children often left school at the age of nine or ten to start work. The fact that schools were run predominantly by the churches for their congregations, may in part be responsible for the large attendances and influence the churches had within the communities at that time. The Education Act of 1861 greatly reduced their power. This Act established an Inspectorate, where schools were visited by inspectors who encouraged improvements in teaching, school management and record keeping. In 1876 William Borland was Chairman of the Local School Board.

In 1803 an Education Act was established to improve the quality of education by enlisting the services of more qualified teachers and offering better conditions of service. The Act stated that each school master school be provided with a house and garden. This may account for the next parish school in Stonehouse to be built in Boghall Street, about 1808, with a room and kitchen house above for the school master. Originally a single storey building, Camnethan Street School had a second storey added in 1898. One of the first headmasters to teach there was 'Dominie' Robert S. Wotherspoon (also session clerk) who died in 1891. Some may still remember Mr Alexander Anderson who succeeded Mr Wotherspoon and retired in 1924.

In 1836 there were five schools in the parish attended by some three hundred scholars. Two of these schools were subscription schools. A new parish school was erected a short distance from the original school in Townhead Street in the year 1853, later enlarged in 1870, 1881 and 1912. A house was also built for the teacher near the Free Manse, called Sauchrie Cottage. The new Education Act of 1872 introduced a revolution in the educational affairs of parishes, where control of education was handed over to the state. Responsibility for the parish schools and burgh schools were transferred to the newly created School Boards, which later gained control of many non-parochial schools. This Act also instructed that attendance at school should be compulsory for all children between the age of five and thirteen, although exceptions were made for children over ten, whose family circumstances made it necessary for them to find work.

The school board of Stonehouse acquired Greenside School formerly a subscription school, built in 1853, and then converted it into an infant school. In 1895, children who were five year old, were taught at Greenside School which consisted of two rooms. Both teachers were women, and thus, it became known as the 'lady school'. The children were taught reading, writing and arithmetic until they reached the age of transferring to either Camnethan Street or Townhead Street where they were taught other subjects such as geography and history. Greenside later became a school for woodwork and domestic sciences.

The Free Kirk School in Hill Road was opened in the year 1851 and was run by the congregation until 1880, when it was disposed of under the Free Church of Scotland School Properties Act, 1878, and became private property. The school board rented Hill Road School from the proprietor for one year intending to build a new school but their lease expired and they rented the E.U. Church until the new school was erected at Townhead Street in 1881. Unfortunately Hill Road School was destroyed by fire during November 1936.

Children of the Victorian era were expected to buy their own books, and it was common place for books to be handed down through the family as was so often done with clothing. On the wall at the corner of Sidehead Road can be seen quite a number of worn grooves in the stonework, caused by children sharpening their pencils to be used on slate.

Few will remember one of Stonehouse's most popular headmasters Alexander McIntosh who earlier in his life was fortunate to escape from the Tay Bridge disaster in 1879. Initially employed as a monitor he was promoted to an appointment at the Free Church School in Hill Road, before being appointed to headmaster of Townhead Street in 1882. Mr McIntosh was a very active member of the community before retiring in 1914.

Another popular teacher who lives today near Ferniegair, at the age of eighty nine, is Kit Small. Kit, born in Swinhill, trained at Jordanhill College and graduated at Glasgow University in 1927, before being appointed to Camnethan Street School on October 3rd 1929 an transferred to Townhead Street four years later. She retired in June 1971. Kit was Stonehouse's longest serving teacher, and is often fondly remembered for her teaching, especially poetry and prose which she still recites to this day. My wife and I regularly visit Kit and her sister Jen (ninety three), where we are often held captivated by her knowledge of 'auld stanis' and her memories of the village as a child and teacher.

During the 1930s and indeed into the late 1940s, many children were still without footwear. For this reason a 'boot fund' was established to provide footwear for all children. Attendances at the schools were affected all year round. Vaccinations were not as common as they are in todays schools and, thus, diseases such as measles, mumps, flu, diptheria and scarlet fever were not uncommon. During the winter these ailments took their toll, as did the weather which badly affected transport and road conditions. In the summer, pupils were often granted absence for 'potato gathering' or to help with the harvest.

Until the late 1940s all Catholic and Protestant children mixed together at both Camnethan Street and Townhead Street schools. During the Second World War many children from all over Glasgow, including Carntyne and later Clydeside, were evacuated to Stonehouse and matched with appropriate families for the duration of their stay. All of the initial intake (229 from St. Thomas's) were Catholic and were used to being taught in separate schools in Glasgow. These children also brought with them their own teachers and a priest, who insisted they were taught separately. The priest was surprised to find that in Stonehouse all children were taught together. When the war concluded, the priest then pursued having Catholic children transferred to St. Mary's in Larkhall and St. Patrick's in Strathaven, where today the majority of our Catholic children are taught. Many children could not settle into their new surroundings and were either redeployed or returned to Glasgow. During the war years Alexander Anderson was headmaster of Camnethan Street School and Robert Leggate, a former pupil of his, was the headmaster of Townhead School.

Camnethan Street School, more affectionately known as the 'Dominie' (Scots for school master) was closed in 1947 with the children being transferred to Townhead School. It was briefly opened on occasion while renovations took place to Townhead School in 1950/51 and as a dinner hall and overflow of classes from Townhead. In 1956 the school was sold to the Congregational Church and was demolished to make way for another housing development in March 1995.

Today in education, classes of thirty are regarded as too large, yet in the 1950s, classes of over fifty were common, such as in 1958, when there were four classes of such a size. With pupils of all ages still being taught in Stonehouse, school rolls were large. The logbook of Townhead Street School in 1958 had 530 pupils on the roll. It wasn't until June of 1953 that both Camnethan Street School and Greenside School removed all its pupils to Townhead School to be taught under one roof. The growth of the village after the Second World War, and the developments of the gas, electric and Westmains housing schemes, found there was a need for a second school in the village. Thus, in August 1979 Newfield Primary was opened.

Adult Recreation

In Stonehouse, as in so many villages throughout Scotland, social life and entetrainments were arranged almost entirely by voluntary organisations. The lack of transport and leisure facilities within the village accounted for many and varied social activities which were all well supported. Leisure time for villagers was enjoyed by participating in minor sports such as bowling, curling or fishing.

Curling was especially popular in Stonehouse, played at the Tilework Park. It is not clear how this winter sport originated. Freezing conditionscould last up to four weeks, which allowed formation of a league with regular fixtures, against neighbouring parishes. Originally it may have been simply throwing stones on ice, shaped like quoits, there being old stones niches for the finger and thumb; but if this was the case the game must have undergone considerable improvement since then. At what time the game was instituted in the parish it is hard to say. A club was formed in connection with the Royal Caledonian Curling Club of Scotland. The system was formerly to play with eight persons on each side, one stone each, but then changed to four on each side with two stones each. In 1896 the president of the club was Archibald Shearer.

While curling was the winter pursuit, quoits and kyles were summer pastimes. Kyles derives from the french word quilles, and was a favourite sport of James IV. In Stonehouse it was especially popular with the weavers, quoits more commonly associated with the miners. In his book 'Hame' George Wilson, quotes his grandfather George 'Wheelie' saying

> *We had a hawthorn hedge bordering our garden with Kirk Street, and, in the old, popular game of kyles played among men folk, this stretch with head and run from Greenside corner, made the best rink in the village centre.*

The objective of the game was to attain a predetermined number of shots which was generally forty-one for competition matches, and thirty-one for local friendlies. The winner was usually the best of five or seven sets. The pitch had to be a surfaced, well trodden, common or roadway with at least thirty yards in at least two directions from the 'head' or centre where the kyles were set. Manse Road was a popular venue for these events. Kyles were made of hardwood, fifteen inches in length and three inches in diameter. A set comprised of nine kyles, eight alike, the master kyle was named the 'pape' or 'head' and controlled the others. The nine were set on their feet, in a three kyle square formation, with the 'head' in the centre. Shots were played by rolling or throwing a wooden ball of football proportions. The spacing of the kyles such that the ball could be thrown through the head without disturbing the set. The art lay in making the correct fall to suit the player's score, which advanced one with each falling kyle. Opponents started from a marking in the vicinity of the head. The toss-winner took the ball, and gripping it with both hands, had the option of throwing at his discretion at any length, in any direction, away from the head, and where it rested was the starting mark. This point thereafter was called 'the flittin'. From the 'flittin' each opponent, in turn, threw or rolled the ball towards the head, only one ball was used, the first objective being to reach the head, or as near as possible to it, and the resting place marked. The head was only occasionally disturbed by the first throw. From there the kyles were registered and replaced, and the player allowed his second throw from a three yards distance. Each player had two throws only, then returned to the 'flittin' to recommence.

George Wilson states that the rules varied from area to area but the above rules were generally accepted among the inter-parish challenge matches. By the establishment and popularity of the Bowling Club, kyles soon gave way to the ever changing leisure pursuits within the village. Tarmac and pavements were also responsible for the downfall of kyles. The Bowling Club was formed in 1857 and the original green was situated at Lochpark in Kirk Street before moving to its present location at Vicars Road.

Quoiting was another favourite pastime in the parish played by many but now played mainly by children. The aim was to throw a 10lb band of steel with consistent accuracy on to a clay-embedded steel pin twenty one or eighteen yards distant, in a 'sixty one' shot game, of four hours duration. This sport was still popular in the 1920s. There still exists a pitch at Birkenshaw, which is used regularly by a quoiting club in Larkhall.

Other recreational pursuits were cricket, played at Newfield as far back as 1858 and lawn tennis, introduced in the 1880s. A new cricket club was formed in 1883, called 'The Royal' Cricket Club. Tennis was played at Holm Farm belonging to Mr Shearer. The first patron of the club was Mrs Jackson of Hill Cottage. A cycling club was established in the nineteenth century, sending representatives to the World Championships in 1897.

There was was once at Millholm and with held there annually, with the the custom to run for the prize of a silver bell. There is also a tradition that there was a race course at one time from Woodlands out through the 'half-acre' and through the village.

In 1887, there was a team under the name of the Royal Football Club playing at Newfield. Pre First World War there were football teams called Violet and Albion, the latter never reformed after the great war. Violet, however, did reform changing their name to Stonehouse United until their demise around 1925 when they renamed themselves Stonehouse Violet. The team formerly played at Holm Park before moving to their present location at the Tilework Park around 1956. Lately their greatest success was in 1978, when almost the whole village turned out at Hampden Park to see them reaching the Junior Cup Final, being beaten 1-0 by Bonnyrigg Rose.

Most locals know of the golf course which existed at the Holm Farm during the First World War but what many may not know is that our first golf course was at West Town Farm, as far back as 1896. The following is an extract from the *Hamilton Advertiser* reporting on the opening.

> **June 1896**
> *The formation of a golf club in Stonehouse is now an accomplished fact, and considering the class of membership that have joined or signified their intention to do so, it is evident that the club has come to stay. A suitable course has been found near West Town Farm. Several holes have already been got, and others are in formation. Good play has been got, and in course of time we may be proud of the position Stonehouse Golf Club will hold in golfing circles.*

Unfortunately the 'Watstoune' Golf Club was only to survive until August the following year. The golf club at Holm Farm was inaugurated in 1910 and opened in 1912. It was a nine hole course and its steep banks provided quite an obstacle for many. The first president of the club was Robert Rule and the captain was David Stirling. The Club ceased to exist not long after the First World War.

A popular pastime in the village during the late nineteenth and early twentieth century was beekeeping. On 4th December 1944 the Stonehouse and District Beekeepers Association was formed, headed by President Joseph Brown. Meeting in the Dramatic Club Hall in King Street the club grew from strength to strength, competing against neighbouring clubs and exhibiting their produce. In 1951 the secretary of the Beekeeper Association was the ex-Station Master James Rattray. The clubs most notable success came in the years 1956 and 1957 when a team consisting of Messers Millar, Thomson, Rattray and Johnston won the McClymont Cup. Beekeeping in Stonehouse was on the decline during the late 60s, with poor harvest years and many of their older members dying. The organisation was finally wound up on 20th June 1973. From an extract of the *Hamilton Advertiser* it is clear to see the obvious attraction to beekeeping.

> **October 1968** (by Hugh Burns)
> *In the early hours of the morning, the hives were loaded onto the horse and cart for the long haul to the heather moors. Various stops were made on the way to refresh both man and horse. The arrival at the heather, with the resultant release of the bees, was a tricky job calling for an alertness of mind and body which had not been impaired by strong refreshment! In the ensuing battle the bees usually emerged as victors with the beekeepers in full retreat!*
>
> *Then began the trek home with all the temptations of the roadside inns to attract the travellers. By this time the responsibility of getting the party home safely by the late evening, lay with the horses rather than the drivers.*

Youth Recreation

In general the Victorian working-class child had far less time for play than his twentieth century counterpart. Until 1863, young children could be employed up to twelve hours per day in factories. Even after the 1872 Education Act, many children continued to work part time, leaving few moments for leisure. For the children of the more affluent families there would be long hours in the nursery playing with handmade. There were few of the prepackaged entertainments we have today, and there was much more scope for imagination and improvisation in children's play whatever their class.

As a child I was fortunate enough to have an eventful and adventurous life, mixed with happy recollections of my early school years at Townhead. Class breaks were spent playing games, such as Statues, Under Arm Tig, British Bull Dog, What's the Time Mr Wolf and my personal favourite Dead Man's Fall, whereby participants had the chance to choose death by various weapons and make a spectacular plunge from a great height to their death. This game was the scene of many Oscar winning performances, the most stupendous being death by hand grenade. Fortunately none of my wounds were fatal, though I did suffer the odd case of concussion.

There have been many youth organisations in Stonehouse, supporting a wide range of activities, including the Boys' Brigade, the Girls' Brigade, the Girl Guides and the First Stonehouse Scout Troup. The Scout Troop was first established in 1913 and re-established after the war in 1928. The Boys' Brigade was established in April 1894 by Rev. James Wyper Wilson and their first captain was James Curr. In the 1950s there was a small company of the Army Cadet Force in the village of approximately twenty six boys, which formed part of the 4th Lanarkshire Battalion.

Many of these organisations still thrive within the community as well as two excellent athletic clubs which are regularly producing junior internationalists. Also established in recent times was the Stonehouse Youth Forum which was responsible for the return of the *Stonehouse Lantern* magazine for over three years. (The original paper was produced in 1868 as an election publicity paper but lasted only a few months).

Fairs

Not a great distance from Castlehill, on the Spittal Road, lies 'Grossyett Knowe'. The origins of this name are uncertain but in trying to unravel its meaning it is probably easier to break the word up and decipher each section separately. A 'knowe' is quite simply a hilltop. When researching the word 'yett' in a Scots dictionary the word is described as—'a natural pass between hills' (Gateway). Alternatively, Grossyett may have been a corruption of the Scots word 'Groset' meaning—'an agricultural fair'. This is an attractive theory as Grossyett Knowe lies right in the farming heartland not far from where the present agricultural shows take place. Agricultural fairs were well known to have taken place here going back several centuries.

Markets in the early days formed a substantial part of the village income, from the buying and selling of cattle and toll charges received from traders outwith the parish. Market days were also the time to pay half yearly accounts between farmers and tradesmen, as well as servants changing hands. These markets were known as the feeing days. With improvements in transport, fair days' in rural Lanarkshire became very popular, bringing in day visitors from the surrounding towns and Glasgow. Growers and craftsmen brought their produce to be sold and anyone caught selling or buying outside the markets was fined. Parents and children always dressed in their best clothes and their houses and doorsteps were painted in honour of the 'fair day'.

Rev. Hugh Dewar's *Statistical Account of Stonehouse* of 1836 containing interesting information of the people attending fairs of the past.

> *In a moral and religious point of view, the inhabitants of the village of Stonehouse (which contains a population of nearly 1600 souls) are, with a few exceptions, an industrious, sober, and religious people, nowise addicted to the many vices of the inhabitants of villages of a similar population throughout the kingdom,—such as excessive drinking, swearing, and fighting. Quarrelling and fighting are seldom or never heard of ; and though there are three well attended fairs held in the village yearly, yet many pass over without the slightest appearance of a quarrel.*

During the nineteenth century there were three main fairs, on 28th May, the last Wednesday in July and 28th November (Martinmas). These days were generally local holidays but by the end of the century were changed to Saturdays. Martinmas was named after St. Martin, the 4th century Bishop of Tours and tutor of Ninian. The May festival is still run today on the third Saturday of the month, and appears to have grown in popularity over the past few years. 1994 saw the return of the Clydesdales to the cattle show. A popular event during the nineteenth century was ploughing matches between local farmers, with as many as thirty two taking part, as was the case in 1878.

Before the establishment of the Agricultural Society in 1858, the parishes of Stonehouse and Dalserf held combined shows, generally at the Grossyett Knowe. Nowadays the Agricultural Show is primarily a show of livestock from the surrounding farms. The May and November fairs of the past were mainly for the buying and selling of cattle. The July fair, once the largest in the country, was a cattle market but was principally a wool market. These fairs could often last for days and were very popular with the children of the village. In the latter end of the nineteenth century, 'Pinder Ord's Circus' came to the village, with performing dogs, hens, elephants, horses and trapeze artists. The circus was always attended by large audiences. Unfortunately, many of these fairs attracted pickpockets and vagrants:

> *Hamilton Advertiser* May 1897
> **PICKPOCKETS**
> *These light fingered gentry were in evidence at the show on Wednesday, and three of them were caught.*

During the First World War trotting was popular at the shows, as was the hobby horse which came with the fairground rides. The 'bearded lady' was one of the more peculiar attractions at that time.

The Grossyett Knowe is a common place to find amateur archaeologists with metal detectors. Reminders of these great fairs can still be unearthed, giving a better insight as to what took place at these events.

The first Gala Day on record was Saturday 19th June 1948. The chairman of the Gala and the County Council of that time was Robert Brodie who served from 1948-52. The Gala Queen during this period was 'Queen of the Roses'. In 1948 Anne Elliot was Queen and her Champion was James Aitken. The venue of the crowning ceremony was the bandstand in the public park, where the pipe band played regularly. The Queen and Court visited Stonehouse Hospital after the crowning ceremony, a tradition still upheld. On Gala Day, inscribed commemorative medals were presented to the Queen and Court. Food rationing was still in force so pplication to the food office was essential to produce supplies for the large gathering of people who witnessed the ceremony in the public park. Stonehouse Merchants' Association presented the committee with a cheque for £50 (reckoned at the time to be a magnificent sum) to set in motion an annual Gala Day as the initial one was deemed a great success. Sports had to be cancelled this year because of adverse weather conditions.

Gala Days from 1949-1952 followed more or less the same format, but lapsed from 1953-1958. In 1959 a meeting was called to revive the event, to be held in May, changing the name of the Queen of the Roses, to the May Queen, and the boy attendant to Herald. Mr Jack McEwan was chairman from 1959-1964. The May Queen originates from an ancient Celtic festival. A horse drawn open Landau was hired from the Co-op to transport the May Queen to the park. The Stonehouse Silver Band and Larkhall Silver Band were regulars at the Gala

Days. The Stonehouse Pipe Band had only a few members during this time. The Tilework Park, Union Street was used for the Crowning Ceremony but there were problems with the park being waterlogged and, on one occasion Guy Hamilton's field off Udston Mill Road had to be used as an emergency.

Before 1963 the boys had worn Elizabethan costumes, but by 1964 they had converted to kilts. The Gala Day then lapsed from 1965-1974. From 1974 -1992 the Gala Day was held in the public park before returning once again to the Tilework Park. This festival has been thriving over the past few years, and is one of very few gala days in Lanarkshire. Having been chaired by Fred McDermid for ten years, the festival committee under the auspices of the community council is now chaired by Andrew Wilson, aided by a hard working committee.

Musical Entertainment

Stonehouse Pipe Band

The Pipe Band was formed on 11th October 1899 under Pipe Major Hector McInnes, accompanied by his two sons on drums. They formed the foundations of the band. It grew steadily, practising originally in Townhead School. It was a competing band and had their most notable success in 1909 when it set a world record winning the Argyle and Lauder Shieilds at the Cowal Games. This was undoubtedly their most successful period, winning many trophies.

The band was self supporting and relied on fund raising events and members contributions to pay for instruments, uniforms and music. In 1935, they appealed for financial support from the community to buy a new set of uniforms. Throughout the next year, various fund raising events took place and they obtained their new uniforms in June 1936. Originally the band wore the Macgregor tartan but later changed to the Hamilton Dress Tartan in the 1930s, donated by Mrs Janet Millar of Tinto View (Mrs Millar was a sister of Alexander Hamilton of Kidderminster who gifted the public park to the village).

The band began to decline around 1939-40. Fierce competition from other bands with financial backing put increasing pressure on the Stonehouse band and they found it difficult to compete. Industrial depression, financial problems and differences of opinion began to cause friction within the band. They broke up several times throughout the years but always reformed again. They finally disbanded around the late 1940s.

Stonehouse Silver Band

Stonehouse Silver Band was founded around 1901-1902. The band was also self-supporting and relied on subscriptions and fund raising events to raise money to buy music, instruments and uniforms. The early years of the band were spent giving local concerts and fund raising events. Throughout the war years they gave concerts for wounded soldiers in hospital and regularly played at the Palace Picture House and the Rex. Also a competing band they were very successful from 1919 and right through the 1920s. In 1919 they won the Scottish Championships and their trombone player James Chalmers was the British Empire Champion Trombonist. They had the reputation of being one of the best bands in Scotland throughout the 1920s.

In the thirties the band began to decline, probably due to the industrial depression, financial problems and a general lack of interest. In 1936 a meeting was called in the band room to discuss the future. Although the members at this time were keen to keep the band going, sadly it did not survive beyond the late 1930s.

Stonehouse Male Voice Choir

Towards the end of 1935, in the work yard of George Wilson (Stonehouse) Ltd. in Green Street, a few of the employees would gather together at lunchtime and sing. They enjoyed this so much that they decided to form a choir in the village. A meeting was held in the Public Hall on 10th January 1936 and Stonehouse Male Voice Choir was established. There were twenty six members originally, all of them local men. The conductor, Robert Chalmers, was one of the original group of men who sang in the yard.

Originally, the choir practised in Townhead School on Monday evenings. However, after some time, the education authority informed the choir that if they wished to continue to use the school, they would have to be under the auspices of the Education Department. This would mean that the Education Department would be involved in the management of the choir and would decide which engagements they would undertake. The choir wished to remain an independent body and so had to move from the school. They changed their practise venue to the Congregational Church and later to Paterson Church where they still practise today.

In the early days, performances were mostly local. The first annual concert was held in January 1937. Throughout the years it has gone from strength to strength. A slight setback was suffered in the 1970s when the number of members fell very low. This was probably due to the development of other forms of entertainment and a general lack of interest. The choir survived this period and now has fifty to sixty members who come from all over Lanarkshire. Performances take them all over Scotland and they have an extensive repertoire. In 1990 they became members of the Scottish Massed Male Voice Choir and appeared on television in a performance from the Glasgow Royal Concert Hall, accompanied by Strathclyde Police Pipe Band and the Scottish CWS Band. The choir is more successful now than ever, and popularity is increasing steadily by year. This year the choir celebrates its sixtieth anniversary.

A' the Airts Burns Club

A popular and growing organisation in the village, A' the Airts Burns Club is among the best and oldest in Scotland today. With regular meetings every month in the Public Institute, the club endeavour to keep alive the memory of Robert Burns the narrative poet, through his song and verse. Records of the club date back to at least 1859, when meetings were held either in the Black Bull Hotel or the Buckshead Inn. At one time called the 'Jolly Beggars' the Burns Club was renamed A' the Airts in the early 70s. Presently chaired by Alex McInnes (Lesmahagow), the club has thrived with an array of talent including singers, recitals, mouth organs, guitars, squeeze boxes, whistles and bodhrans. The club is represented by all ages from eight to eighty promoting the friendship, spirit and character of the village. The Burns Club also play their part in supporting the Scottish whisky industry.

Stonehouse Hospital

Probably the first hospital in the parish was at the Spittal. The house standing there today dates back to at least 1596. During the 17th century the land of Spittal was said to belong to the hospital of Hamilton, St. Thomas Martyr. The word Spittal, Spittel or Spital in Scots means either a charity hospital or a hospice for shelter for travellers. It has been recorded that a convent was once established at the Spittal, but little is known of its history. Notably travellers did indeed seek shelter and refuge on their journey here, under the 'hospitality' of the convent.

St. Anthony's Well is also situated here, dating back to pre-christianity. This well has recently been restored by the Heritage Group but unfortunately the water source was cut off during the surveying of the New Town proposals in the 1970s. Previously said to cure the ailments of horses, the well had two small statues of St. Anthony resting on its top. Evidence supports the theory that a religious was present here at one time.

One peculiar coincidence connected with Stonehouses' Holy wells and the present hospital is that St. Patrick's Well, was said to cure scrofula (tuberculosis of the lymph glands) and consumption (tuberculosis of the lungs) which are diseases that Stonehouse Hospital was originally designed to treat.

In 1778, eighteen children died from smallpox within a few weeks. During the eighteenth century smallpox was said to return every four or five years. Diptheria outbreaks during 1876 and 1884 also resulted in deaths within the parish. These diseases and many others were due to a lack of medical knowledge and poor health awareness, as well as inadequate sanitation.

In 1845 it was generally thought that the life expectancy of a man in the upper class was approximately forty seven years old compared with twenty six years of age for those at the foot of the social ladder. One in four children died within the first year of life. The young and old were particularly at risk. With little medical help or medicine available, they were vulnerable to many illnesses and diseases such as typhus fever, measles, whooping cough, diphtheria, smallpox, dysentery, diarrhoea and cholera. Inadequate nourishment and living conditions did nothing to confront the many ailments. Sleeping arrangements among the weavers also helped spread disease, particularly cholera outbreaks, as it proved, almost impossible to isolate cases. A last factor which may have increased the weavers vulnerability to disease was their liking for alcohol.

In March 1893 the parochial board met with a deputation of the school board and the community to consider the feasibility of erecting a fever hospital for the first division of the Middle Ward on the land of Tofts. This land was donated by the superior Sir Robert Duncan Sinclair-Lockhart of Castlehill.

Tofts was previously Templar lands, as were Woodlands and Cat Castle. Templar, also called Knight Templar was a religious military order of knighthood established in the times of the crusades. Around AD 1120 eight or nine French knights vowed to set up a religious order to protect the Holy sepulchre and escort pilgrims spreading the word of Christianity. As the 'Knights Templar' grew they became a feared powerful army with considerable wealth and properties thoughout Europe. They adopted absolute secrecy to protect all their internal activities, which in turn lead to fear of the templars, especially in France where King Philip IV sought their destruction in the early 1300s. The templars are thought by many to be the ancestors of the Freemasons. In 1694 William Lockhart of Lee was knight, ambassador to France.

In January 1896 Stonehouse Hospital was completed and ready for occupancy. Before its opening the community was invited to examine the hospital and its modern equipment. The hospital when opened provided beds for twenty patients. The architect of the hospital was Alexander Cullen. The innovative sinks designed by Cullen in the hospital were adopted by Sir Arthur Bloomfield for the London hospitals, they were described as "a simple and inexpensive invention that would lighten the drudgery work of the hospital staff, and effectively carry off all germs and diseases". On completion it was said the building was "the best isolation hospital in Scotland", built at a cost of between £5000-£6000. The medical and management staff of the hospital, at its opening were:

Management Officials	Dr. Wilson (County Medical Officer)
	Dr. McLintock
Sanitary Inspector	Mr Dobson
	Mr Stewart (Assistant)
Medical Attendant	Dr. McLean
Matron	Miss Stevenson and her staff

There was also a Mr Mckenzie working in the hospital but his remit is unclear. Dr. Sutherland was one of the first doctors at the sanatorium, followed by Dr. Smith and Dr. Pettigrew, who both served in the hospital during the war years.

In 1900 the hospital's provisional needs were tendered out locally, including an ambulance hire service from Hugh D. Burns. This service was horse drawn, with a pole sited in the hospital for tethering the horses.

In both the First and Second World Wars, wards were added to the hospital to cope with emergency services and wounded soldiers recuperating. Members of the Canadian army were also billeted here for a time. Some people may remember that they were responsible for the blowing up of the old Cander Bridge in 1942. During the Second World War sick parades of the military were seen every day except Sunday. At one period a ward was used for German, Italian and Polish prisoners receiving treatment for their wounds.

Many expressed their gratitude for their excellent treatment, as many feared they would have lost limbs, had they been treated at home. One Polish prisoner is said to have shot himself in the foot to avoid being repatriated, as he was wanted in his own country for bank robbery.

A popular visitor to the hospital shortly after the First World War was Mrs Ferrie, on whose ice cream van Henry McFarlane remembers working as a boy. Some may also recall the slaughterhouse (Robert Rankin in charge) sited across from the bus stop at Violet Cresent, where storage sheds now stand.

Before nationalisation the hospital and its staff were paid by the County. In the years 1935-1936 a nurse would expect to have been paid £2 per month, with half a day off per week and a day off per month. This rose to £3 in 1936-37.

In 1942 there were seventeen wards full of patients. Many TB patients were evacuated to fever hospitals at Dalserf and Calderbank to allow for military casualties. Pavilion one was said to have been used as an officers mess. Pavillion two and wards one to six were accommodated by T.B. patients, while wards seven to fourteen were for general patients. Pavillion three was used for treating ENT patients (Ears, Nose and Throat). After the war had ended the hospital became a General Unit, used as a training institution, from 1949. Several nurses from Germany came here for training during this time. A new Out-Patients Department and theatre were opened and many more clinics held. Casualty and X-Ray departments functioned on a twenty four hour 'On Call' basis and Pavillion one was converted into a Laboratory. After Nationalisation in 1947 many changes took place including an increase in the number of staff.

Throughout the war years and the 1950s fund raisers and charity events were especially popular, to produce much needed money for the hospital and local needs. These events were well organised and attended. On occasion celebrities (Stanley Baxter in September 1958) were invited to take part. In 1950 improvements were made, such as, laying concrete paths, erecting iron railings, removing some trees and widening the eastern entrance. The following year improvements were made to several wards and the nursing home to bring them in line with other hospital facilities throughout Scotland. In 1954 chest operations were being carried out in the hospital as part of the ever increasing service being provided, including ENT and eye surgery.

Since the change in government policy, allowing hospitals to manage their own affairs, the hospital has gained Trust Status. However, there has been a gradual run down of services, especially the emergency services which no longer function twenty four hours per day. The hospital is expected to close by the end of the century due to new facilities and money being invested in Hairmyres Hospital, East Kilbride and Netherton, Wishaw.

The Stanis Witches

Witchcraft was common place in Scotland between the sixteenth and eighteenth centuries. Practising witchcraft was a criminal offence in Scotland until 1736. Between 1479 and 1722, 17,000 people, mostly women, were tortured or put to death. The estates of those convicted went to the Crown, thus witch hunting was a profitable business for those prosecuting. The last recorded burning of a suspected witch was Janet Horne in 1727.

The legend of the Stonehouse witches is well known in the village. Neighbouring parishes were constantly attributing accidents and strange occurrences with local women. Traders and visitors when passing through the village would carry branches of rowan tree, as a charm to protect them from the evil powers of the witches. At fairs many of those in competition with local opponents would carry potions of rowan tree to keep the spirits at bay. Some say that the witches are unable to leave the parish, for it was known that witches are unable to cross running water. In the 1850s a gentleman writing in the *Hamilton Advertiser* stated that many local people in the village, had in the past, planted Rowan trees in their gardens to ward off the powers of evil.

One elderly man was said to take advantage of other villages superstitions of Stonehouse folk. This happened when one day when he was making his way to Millholm Dam, where a curling match was being played. Watching them from a distance, the players were put off by his presence believing he had sinister connections with the witches. He played upon their suspicions, and from a small box released, what appeared to the curlers, to be small white creatures to run about. In fact they were white mice.[1]

In the days when a bell tolled in the old jail, the bell ringer (known only by the initials J.C.) claimed that when he climbed the stairs to ring the bell at night, witches would grip his legs and pull.[1]

Today witchcraft is still common place, practiced without the persecution of the eighteenth century. Nowadays we are more likely to be critical or dismissive of strange occurrences of the supernatural. Despite this there have been several 'strange occurrences' and superstitions that are present today. The most commonly known 'ghost story' is that of the eerie sounds of trains in the area of Whinriggs, on the Westmains Estate. Although the line closed in the late 1960s, many people, unknown to one another, have said they have heard the sound of a train passing in the night. Probably the best recording of this was by a woman from Whinriggs, who said her two year old son, cried out in the middle of the night claiming that a train was coming through his bedroom wall. His mother initially dismissed this as a nightmare. The boy is now nine years old and still claims to hear and see the train. It wasn't until recently the woman found out that the railway line goes virtually past her house. It is rare for there to be apparitions of trains, as most ghostly appearances are in the form of living beings. It may be that the number of deaths on the line, may have caused this strange phenomenon to occur. There have been many accidents involving the shunting of trains. A woman, in August 1882, released from an asylum, committed suicide by laying her head on

Reference: 1 Stonehouse, Traditional and Historical

the line, placing a handkerchief over her face and awaiting the 5pm from Glasgow, which proceeded to sever her head.

An area where there have been a number of ghost stories is the River Avon. Fishermen's tales are famous all over, but the sheer number of unusual sightings cannot be disregarded in every case as imaginary. The river has been the scene of many deaths, either by drowning in its perilous pools or mining on its banks. During the eighteenth century there were tidal floods, sweeping away bridges in their path. Only last year I was told of a fisherman who had been fishing on the Avon, when he noticed a man in old working clothes, watching him from the opposite bank. At first the fisherman thought nothing of it, until the man began walking towards him. The unusual thing about this was, that he was said to have been walking on top of the water, then as he approached, simply disappeared.

Another case of disappearing ghosts was on Manse Road near the old kirk yard. In this case a woman was travelling into the village one morning when she noticed a horse with a woman riding side-saddle across the road. The woman on the horse was dressed in Victorian clothing and the horse's legs were cut short as if it were walking through water on the road. Again the apparition disappeared without trace. Why this ghostly figure should appear is uncertain, but the horses legs being shorter, may be explained by the constantly changing levels in the ground. In the North of England for instance, Roman legions have been seen in similar circumstances, walking through moors, with their legs cut off, due possibly to agricultural land improvements and the level of the land altering with the ever changing environment.

An old superstition that still exists today is that of the 'Blood Stone'. Told to me many years ago, I neither believed the story nor found evidence of its existence until of late. As a child I had been told of a gravestone in the old graveyard with a hole in it. When inserting a finger in this hole it was said to come out covered in blood. I dispelled this as a myth of the past, until out walking one summer day in the graveyard. To my amazement and by accident, I found a hole in a stone, more commonly known as the Covenanters' stone. The hole is located on top of the stone directly below the mouth of a stone carved skull. When I found the stone I immediately remembered the tale told to me as a boy and hesitantly stuck my finger in the hole. Pulling out my finger it was red, not with blood but with red ochre dust. This is due to a vein of red ocre running through the grey sandstone inside. When it was raining, however, the red ochre must have given the impression of 'blood' to the younger and more imaginative mind.

Advertiser Extracts

The *Hamilton Advertiser* has been invaluable in recording the events of the latter half of the nineteenth century and the war years. Not only has this information provided me with a wealth of local historical knowledge, it has also recorded many entertaining, amusing and extraordinary incidents that have occurred in the past.

From its humble beginnings in 1856, as a two page spread, the *Hamilton Advertiser* has provided local organisations with the opportunity to advertise and inform the public of the varied events and meetings taking place in the village. Considering the size of the population, the village is well voiced in the local news section, compare with other larger towns in the district.

During the 1970s a newspaper known locally as the *Larkhall and Stonehouse Gazette* was circulating, providing the village with a more in depth knowledge of local news. Of special interest in this newspaper were several articles, written by Jean T. Leishman on the history of the parish. Jean was the local correspondent for the paper and has always taken a keen interest in our history and that of the church of St.Ninian's. Her knowledge and interest have often given me inspiration and encouragement in my own research into our historical background. Unfortunately for the *Gazette*, its lifespan was short lived and it ceased in the late 1970s.

In April 1994 a small free advertising paper was established by Alan Kerr in Strathaven, known initially as the *Strathaven and Stonehouse Standard*, it was renamed the following year as *The Avondale Standard* to encompass a wider readership. This paper is a valuable asset to many community organisations for promoting events and attracting new members. Many of the Stonehouse articles are written by the local correspondent for the paper, Andrew Clark. The business is now located in Lochpark Industrial Estate, Stonehouse and provides the village with a worthy alternative to the *Advertiser*.

The following are some of the more interesting and extrodinary occurrences from extracts from the *Hamilton Advertiser*.

December 1892
DARING HIGHWAY ROBBERY NEAR STONEHOUSE
On Saturday afternoon, one of the most daring highway robberies ever attempted in the county was committed between Stonehouse and Larkhall. Mr Cunningham, agent of the Union Bank at Larkhall, attends the Stonehouse branch of the bank on Saturdays. There was an extra amount of business on Saturday last, as that was the half yearly rent-day of General Lockhart's tenants and feu'ars. Business being over, Mr Cunningham, along with one of the clerks, drove homeward in an open conveyance in which were three bags one of which contained money to the extent of £3000 and others a ledger, cheques, &c. When at the part of the bridge which spans the Cander water, and at the place known as "The Cut", he was attacked by three men who came out of the wood, masked and armed with revolvers. One of them seized the horses head and presented a revolver at Mr Cunningham, while the other jumped onto the conveyance, also presenting a revolver, and exclaimed "The gold, the gold, or you are dead in a moment". A struggle ensued in the course of which Mr Cunningham stuck to the bag with the gold, and bore the mask from the man's face, but he managed to escape, carrying off one of the bags containing the documents. The banker immediately drove back to Stonehouse, and informed the police of the affair, which, on being noised abroad created a great sensation. The daring attack was noticed at no great distance by a number of miners on their way from their day's work, but they do not appear to have taken in the unusual situation, although, their evidence is likely to be of invaluable use in bringing the desperados to justice. Sub-Inspector Rodger being about on duty at Ferniegair, Constable James was the man to whom the report of the occurrence was conveyed. On driving to the scene, he found about a dozen miners standing on the road and they accompanied him into the wood in search of the robbers and their booty but failed to find any trace of them. Meanwhile, information got mooted abroad, pointing strongly to two miners, Thomas Summers (27), residing in Camnethan Street, and Alexander Brown (24), Hill Road, as being likely suspects in connection with the robbery. During the afternoon, they had been in the hostelry where Mr Cunningham stabled, and the landlord recalled that one of them had been out about the back of the yard three or four times obviously to pick up information as to the bankers time of leaving. They are further alleged to have been seen on the road leading to the scene of the robbery, and after all was over one of them is said to have been noticed stalking behind a tree in the Lockhart plantation on Hamilton Farm. This circumstantial evidence led to their apprehension by Sub-Inspector Rodger in the course of the evening.

Superintendent Dods arrived later from Hamilton, several constables from Larkhall having previously come on the scene, and a search took place, when there were found a mask similar to those used at fancy balls, an old breech loaded horse pistol which could not have been loaded, waterproof capes and slouched hats, said to be similar to those worn by the accused after their return from America a couple of years ago. In this connection, it is asserted that their leaving for America was coincident with the Stonehouse Station being broken into, but in view of several unfounded stories abroad concerning them, this is probably no more than coincidence. They came back to this country together, and though Brown afterwards went to Australia he returned to Stonehouse some four months ago. The two men were companions and their neighbours and the police unite in describing them as "bad characters". At the same time, they do not hitherto appear to have had any very serious accusations brought home to them.

On Monday, the two accused were taken before Sheriff Davidson at Hamilton, and after being judicially examined were committed to prison pending enquiry. Since then, the Procurator Fiscal has been engaged in examining witnesses with the view to reporting to Crown Counsel. A search party was organised on Wednesday, with the result that the missing bag was found at the mouth of the Cander Water where it joins the Avon. It was buried in two feet of earth, and was found by Robert Millar, Boghall Street, and Constable Cameron, Strathaven. It was taken to the Bank, and after being examined by the clerk, was handed over to the police. Nothing seems to have been taken out of it. Much excitement has been caused by the daring attempt, and the trial of the two suspected men awaited with much interest.

> *Whatever happened to these 'desperados' I do not know, but the story certainly makes interesting reading. You get the impression these men while in America fancied themselves as 'outlaws' and so in returning decided to re-enact their fantasy, complete with cowboy hats and rob the banks payroll being transported by coach. The closest modern day Stonehouse came to highway robbery was in the mid-seventies when the West Mains estate was nearing completion. One of Ginestri's ice cream vans couped over near the entrance to the estate, shedding its load of sweets across the road, and before aid was on the scene children from nearby had escaped with most of the confectionery!*

September 1881
DARING FREAK
A quarry labourer named Hardy laid a wager with a chimney sweep on Saturday evening that he would ascend the two storey house of Mr Hamilton, Hamilton Farm, without a ladder and walk along the ledge of the roof. Although under the influence of liquor, he climbed up the water pipe, and after reaching the roof performed several gymnastic feats on the ridge of such a daring character that the people who had assembled at The Cross were terrified to look at him. He descended unhurt.

October 1860
LARGE TURNIPS
We have been shown a white turnip, grown on the farm of Mr Allan Allison, Gozzelton, Stonehouse, weighing with shaw, 21 lb. and measuring 3 feet in circumference. In the same field there are many others equally large.

November 1861
HYPOCHONDRIACISM
The effects which this unhappy disease produces on the mental system are in many cases exceedingly ridiculous. A short time since an individual was pointed out to us who, at certain seasons of the year, imagines himself, by some singular metamorphosis, transformed into a teapot—the left arm, curved inwards below the armpit being the handle, while the other extended, forms the spout! But a more amusing instance was related to us the other day of a man who constantly labours under the impression that he is a barley-pile, and at sight of a hen becomes terrified, and immediately takes to his heels!

February 1860
STRONG DRINK
A correspondent sends the following—Sir,—By seeing the article headed "The Church and the sellers of strong drink", in your last, I take courage from it to prove in some measure its truth. I attend the prayer meetings in the Free Church here sometimes. One night I heard a request read out for prayer, from a man who had experienced the evils of strong drink. "That the publicans might see the necessity of giving up their soul-destroying hell-filling trade"—(such were the words). Every church here has members connected with the trade, and the most of the ministers give encouragement to it by being non-abstainers. Now, nothing has been done yet by the churches to withdraw their support from, or discountenance the trade; and so long as that is the case, such prayers, to my thinking, are but a solemn mockery to the Most Highest God. By giving the above a place in your columns, you will much further the cause of truth, yours, & C., A lover of Consistency

April 1883
A FREAK OF NATURE
This week there was seen a singular freak of nature in the shape of a monster calf belonging to Mr John Muir, King Street, Stonehouse. It seems to be perfectly developed, with two comely formed distinct heads and necks that join the breast. The forelegs, from the joint, are in the shape of the hind legs. When killed it was also found to have two stomachs. This is considered one of the most singular cases of the kind known in this district.

February 1858
PUFF! PUFF!
Sir,—It strikes me very forcibly in reading the communication from Strathaven in the columns of your newspaper, That if our Strathaven friends have the talent they know it; if any cleverness—they know it; They puff themselves in a manner truly astonishing in this enlightened age. Verily, who is like us? We've cash we've had dons o' ministers, and still have them—we've gingerbread far-famed we've calves, stots, and bulls, equal to none—we've lawyers, weavers, and dominies, a host of young students promising to outstrip their predecessors. All this, and not a word of the castle, the fine romantic scenery around, and the contemplated railway! Again, I say, who is like us? Sandy Bluff

> *We can take from this that there was a great competitiveness between Strathaven and Stonehouse, as there was with Carnwath in later articles. Each village in turn trying to outdo the other, but may it just be that people then were more proud of their village than they are today?*

August 1899
GORED BY A BULL
On Saturday night last, between ten and eleven o'clock, while a number of navvies were returning to the huts, one of them being annoyed at the bellowing of a bull, went into the field with the intention, as he said, of fighting the bull. The enraged animal, rushed at the foolhardy man, and tossed him a distance of about ten yards. The man, whose name is Henry Bradley was rescued from the dangerous position and taken out to the road. Dr. Taylor having been summoned, found that the man had received a wound in the right groin about three inches long and one inch deep, caused by the bull's horn. His injuries having been attended to, he was removed to Hamilton Poorhouse Hospital.

June 1893
A MONSTER EGG
One day last week a minorca hen, belonging to Mr Andrew Loudon, sen., Camnethan Street, laid an egg such has never been seen nor heard of either here or in eccentric places as Carnwath or Uddingston. The dimensions of this overgrown egg are 9in. by 7in., and on being put in the scales by a local grocer the weight was found to be 5 ounces. If all hens were to lay eggs like this there is no doubt but that butcher meat would come down in price.

April 1893
BERRY, THE EX-HANGMAN
James Berry, the ex-hangman, gave one of his lectures on that gruesome subject in the Public Hall on Monday last to a small audience.

There are no recorded hangings in Stonehouse, nor does James Berry show up on the census information we have. The only recorded punishment of crime in Stonehouse was between the years 1760-1790 when a man was punished by a public whipping. Usually you can trace where the hangings took place by looking for 'Gallowhill' on a map.

May 1897
THE WHEELBARROW CRAZE
Strathaven led the way in this silly notion, and Stonehouse has been infected. Mr Buckley was determined that the neighbouring village would not have all its own way, and he decided to beat its champion. This he succeeded in doing on Saturday afternoon, when he pushed or drew a wheelbarrow to Shawsburn and back—a distance of six miles in less time than the Strathaven man did five miles. He is now prepared to meet his Stra'ven friend or any other competitor, and he hopes the challenge may be accepted on an early date.

Tales from the past

BATTLE OF WATERLOO
Family history records the saga of two boys, members of the Murdoch family, late of 32 Hill Road.

One morning in the spring of 1815 James Murdoch entered the weaving shop which he shared with his two sons. "Where is Willie?" he asked of the younger boy James. "He has gone to Larkhall to enlist in the army" was the reply. "Well go down and bring him back James" his father instructed, "tell him we have too much work on hand as it is". Meeting up with his brother on the old Stonehouse to Larkhall road the younger boy delivered the message as advised. "Come on you coward" said Willie. The will of the older boy prevailed and both lads joined up as volunteers in the local infantry regiment, 26th Foot (Cameronians).

On the fatal day, Sunday 18th June 1815, both lads were mortally wounded at the Battle of Waterloo. On the fly leaf of a bible they wrote their names with the only medium available to them—blood. The bible was duly returned to the family by a survivor, as a melancholy relic of the two volunteers who had died for their country. Sunday 18th June 1815 and the irreparable loss to the Murdoch family was long to be remembered in Stonehouse.

Another military related incident, was that of Mrs William Alston who records her father telling her that, as a young boy of ten, witnessed from a tree on Kittymuir Farm in 1745 Bonnie Prince Charlie's Jacobite army marching along Carlisle Road. This can be supported by a recording of the Jacobite army making a temporary stop in Larkhall. It is a misconception that all Jacobites were Highlanders, George Lockhart of Carnwath (descendant of the Lockharts of Castlehill) was adherent to the Jacobite cause in Lowland Scotland. It is also untrue that all Jacobites were Catholic, for they also comprised of Episcopalians and Presbyterians.

THE TWO STONEHOUSE'S AND THE DOWNFALL OF EDWARD II
An interesting link between Stonehouse (Lanarkshire) and Stonehouse (Gloucester) occurred between 1296 and 1328, during a period known in Scotland as the Wars for Independence. The direct line from the first proprietor of the Scottish Stonehouse was Sir William Douglas, a friend and companion of Sir William Wallace. Douglas's son, known in history as "The Good Sir James" Douglas, was the right hand of King Robert the Bruce and was instrumental in hastening the return south of Edward II of England after the Battle of Bannockburn in 1314. Thirteen years later, Edward II visited Berkley Castle, Gloucester, and met an untimely end at the hands of four people, one of whom was John Maltravers, the proprietor of Stonehouse, Gloucester. Walter Fitzgilbert (ancestor of the Dukes of Hamilton) who fought with Bruce at Bannockburn was granted the barony of Cadzow in 1315. Before the Treaty of Union in 1707 the Duke of Hamilton (leader of the country party) was a strong believer in an independent Scotland and had expectations himself of one day becoming King when Queen Anne was unable to provide an heir to the throne.

MINOR MISDEMEANOUR
Not so long ago a local man was in Hamilton Sheriff Court charged with a minor offence. For sake of embarrassment and legal requirements we will call him 'Thomson'. (I hope that's not his real name). As Thomson stood in the dock charged with his offence, he was asked by the court officer his name, to which he replied "Tattie Thomson", the judge with a scornful look to the accused asked him to give his real name before the court, to which he again replied, "Tattie Thomson, your honour". The judge in obvious anger at his arrogance told him if he did not reveal his true name he would be found in contempt of court and fined. The judge once again asked him his name, and the reply from the dock was "Potato Thomson, your honour!". He was duly fined by the judge.

MAIR NOT MAYOR
In August 1937 a Canadian newspaper *The Bassano Recorder* reported an amusing incident involving a former character and native of Boghall Street, Stonehouse. The incident occured during the visit of the King and Queen to Alberta, when the Royal train of blue and silver, consisting of twelve coaches, drew up in Bassano twenty minutes behind schedule. Depite the delay, the King and Queen were impressed by the reception and instructed their aide to call the Mayor to have him presented to them. The aide lent out the window, noticing an elderly man looking on, and asked, "Is the Mayor present?". The old man loooked up smiling and replied, "Well, my names Wullie Mair, but I'm not the Mayor"!

'LIGHT' ENTERTAINMENT
A recent incident, highlighting the character and humour of villagers today, occurred one cold winter's night in Lockhart Street, when an elderly lady had guests over for tea in her home. During the night there was an unexpected powercut, reducing the house to total darkness. The elderly lady and her visitors proceeded outside to investigate the matter, to find that the entire street was without light. The old lady questioned this however, when she said to her friends, "The hale street canny be oot, there's a bus jist away by, wae its lights oan!".

The following extract comes from a correspondent reporting on his visit to Sandford in 1936:

If one could picture another '45 in Scotland with the village of Sandford espousing the modern Jacobite uprising—which Heaven forbid!—this small clachan on the Kype would hold the key position. Why? Look at that direction post at the foot of the village where many motorists in the travelling days of summer dismount to discover their bearings. What village in the county commands so many highways leading north, south, east and west? If Sandford, instead of being pictured in rebellion, were to be imagined exacting toll at the cross roads, as in the bad old days, she would get rich quick, and with her wealth would go all that unsophisticated rurality which is one of her characteristics of those who live and move and have their being within this little cumulation of clean homesteads on Kype-side.

An imaginary campaign
No fewer than five roads fork off at Sandford, and on a stout iron sign-post the various directions are plainly named. That way to Carlisle and South, with all England beyond to plunder! Yon road to Kirkmuirhill and Lanark, where the burghers would be an easy prey to the country-bred Sandfordians! Or this way to Stonehouse, whose capitulation would be a foregone conclusion! Along that fork to Muirkirk, which would be taught to respect the prowess of the men of Kype Water!

Humiliation
Finally, there is the road to Chapelton and Strathaven. Chapelton would be excused, but Strathaven could expect no quarter! There is more than a "gingerbread crumb" to pick with the "Stra'ven Cronies." At the hands of the larger community, Sandford suffers repeated humiliation. How frequently postal communications reach the Kypeside community bearing the legend, "Sandford, by Strathaven." Sandford by Strathaven! What ignorance! How degrading to be known only by proximity to one's neighbour! Is there any other Sandford in Scotland? Not that we know of. True, there's almost a bakers dozen of them in England—but what's England anyway? Caledonia stern and wild knows only one Sandford, and she sits securely where the stream which gives Hamilton its morning bath and quenches its thirst, splashes over a broken and rocky bed, and casts itself over a perpendicular cliff to produce the much visited "Spectacle E'e" falls.

Wha's like us?
Well, but getting down to it, let us say without hesitation, that there are few cleaner villages in the county than Sandford. There has been no sparring of whitewash, which gives colour as well as a preservative to the cottage walls. There are three rows of dwellings, each branching off in a different direction from the others. This gives the village an appearance of roominess and expansiveness. The houses seem all well built and in good order.

The Dominie's domain

A recent addition to the local architecture was a new home for the school master, and the Education Committee acted wisely in their choice both of site and plan. In our village peregrinations we have not come across a more pleasantly situated home for the head teacher than this one flatted bungalow at Sandford beside the school. The dominie was from home when we arrived, and Mrs Headmaster caught us inspecting admiring the exterior of the new schoolhouse. "You can see the inside too," she said, with an inviting smile, and we were charmed with its comfort, its conveinence, and the delectable prospect of the country scenery from the parlour windows. When those features of the home were revealed to us, we could understand the quiet joy and barely suppressed enthusiasm manifested by the good lady in finding, with her husband and her family, such a conveinently built and beautiful home after residence in one of the large industrial areas of the country.

A pivotal point in the social life of Sandford is the annual gala day, when the village from head to toe gives itself to mirth, music, dance and play. Fair Monday is the day—marked red in the local calendar—set apart for this annual festival. Sandfordians the world over return, if not in flesh, at least in the spirit, to their native village on that day. Many natives within convenient distance find the homing instinct on Fair Monday irresistible, and thither they betake themselves to join in the happy reunion, and to renew old but not fogotten associations.

The call of Summer

Sandford is an ideal little summer resort where, in the quietness of its surroundings and the purity and salubrity of its country air, the visitor may find renewal for body, mind and spirit. And in this respect the village is not unknown. Of late years it has increasingly attracted resident visitors, and on the gala day when the season is at its height these temporary dwellers by the Kype take a prominent share in the arranging of the programme for the day. The village is now more accessible and less isolated than it used to be. Prior to the inauguration of the present limited bus services, which links it up with Strathaven, Sandford could only be reached by employing "Shank's naigie" for a few miles if one could not afford a private conveyance.

Lighter in Winter

The village life as a whole was given a new centre when a few years ago, largely by their own efforts, the people built what is known as Waterside Hall, where carpet bowls, concerts and meetings of all kinds help to weld the community more closely together, and to enliven the winter months. The W.R.I. Movement has pleasantly invaded the women's sphere, and brought its ameliorative, helpful and strengthening influence into the home life of the community.

Politics

Prior to the establishment of the County Council in 1889, Stonehouse was represented by local organisations trying to better the working and living conditions of the community. In the nineteenth century the churches were very prominent in the community as most of the schools were run by the churches, thus if you didn't attend church you didn't get an education This meant the churches had a strong voice in the affairs of the village through the Parish Church Board. Other prominent organisations were the School Board, the Mutual Improvement Association and the Building Societies, which pre 1885 numbered fifteen. The Building Societies, in particular, generated much needed finance in providing better housing and facilities for Stonehouse. The Mutual Improvement Association was first started in 1855 with Andrew Thomson as President. The organisation lapsed for a few years before being reorganised under the guidance of Rev. James Laing in 1878. The prime objective of this committee was to bring about improvements to the village, which included the introduction of street lamps.

Prior to the Act of Union Sir John Lockhart represented the county in the Scottish Parliament in 1690 and from 1693-94. Sir Robert Sinclair was the last representative of the county in an independent Scottich Parliament, before its demise in 1707. In December 1889 the first election candidates for the County Council elections were, Major General Lockhart, Robert Naismith and Robert Allan from Glassford. On the 6th May the election was held and Major General Lockhart was elected to represent Stonehouse and Glassford as County Councillor. In 1892 Robert Naismith again challenged the position as County Councillor, but he was defeated again by Major General Lockhart. At the turn of the century Willam Sym was elected county councillor. Not long after the establishment of the County Council, a Parish Council was formed dealing with matters concerning the village at a local level just as the present community council does today. John Frood was elected Chairman in 1898 but died not long after, to be replaced by Alex Borland in 1899. Over the last century many political organisations, including Liberals, the British Socialist Party, the Labour Party and the SNP.

Thomas Wilson	County Councillor		Served 1934-41 Died 1955
G. Thomson	County Councillor		1934-1954 ?
Robert L.Brodie	County Councillor	Lab.	Served 1946 Stepped down 1958
John McEwan	County Councillor	Lab.	Served between 1958-67
Gordon Stewart	County Councillor	Lab.	1970-73
Moyra Burns	County Councillor	Ind.	1967-70 and 1973-76
Fred McDermid	County Councillor	Ind.	1967-1970
William Gracie	District Councillor		Served 1934
David Smith	District Councillor		Served between 1936-41
Nathaniel T.P.W. Mains	District Councillor		Served 1946
Thomas Barr	District Councillor	Lab.	Served between 1958-67
Helen Chalmers	District Councillor	Lab.	1970-73
Mary Ann Gilmour	District Councillor	Lab.	1973-76
Dick Gibb	District Councillor	Lab.	1977-
Bob Wilson	Regional Councillor	Lab.	1975-1990
Jackie Burns	Regional Councillor	Lab.	1990-1996

Stonehouse at War

Before the turn of the century, the local regiment was D (Carluke) Company 9th Lanarkshire Reserve Volunteers. In 1892 the regiment was renamed G Company 9th L.R.V. Previously commanded by Lt. T.G. Smith, the new commander was named as Lt. J.B. Paterson. The company exercised throughout the county, in competition with other companies. At one time there was a firing range at Holm Farm where shooting competitions were held. These events were usually shot at 200, 500 and 600 yards. There were several good marksmen from Stonehouse, including Sergt. William Millar.[1]

In June 1891, the Stonehouse detachment attended a church parade in the village, commanded by Lieutenants Smith and Paterson. There were forty seven present of all ranks, including Major Gray. Only a decade later, many of them were to fight in the Boer War in South Africa.[1]

When First World War came in 1914 the people of Stonehouse rallied together in supporting the armed services overseas and those in need at home. Stonehouse, like most towns and villages, was to suffer great losses of men who gave their lives in the defence of freedom. In the summer of 1994, when the old jail house was being redeveloped the original enlistment register was found, for those enlisting during the First World War including the regiments they served under. This information linked with research from copies of the *Hamilton Advertiser* of the time, is currently held by the Heritage Group. The documentation gives an accurate and sometimes disturbing insight into incidents and casualties experienced during both world wars.

The following is an extract from the *Hamilton Advertiser* at the end of the First World War.

> November 1918
> **VICTORY CELEBRATIONS**
> *On receipt of the news that the Armistice had been signed, steps were immediately taken to celebrate the great event. Flags and bunting were displayed in great profusion, work was stopped, schools were closed, the church bells clanged merrily and the streets were filled with excited joyous crowds. An impromptu pipe band was formed of soldiers and civilians who paraded the streets followed by cheering crowds. In the evening a huge bonfire was lit at the Cross and the silver band played a patriotic programme. On the following days, a high victory demonstration was organised by the Discharged Soldiers and Sailors Federation. The procession paraded the principal streets accompanied by the silver and pipe bands and terminated at the Cross where an enthusiastic meeting was held under the chairmanship of Mr A. McIntosh, F.E.I.S. Speeches extolling the great achievements of the Army and Navy were delivered by Mr A. Anderson M.A. and Mr A. Haddow, M.A.*

Reference: 1 Hamilton Advertiser

During the war years many groups and organisations were formed to aid the war effort. Never before the First World War, had Stonehouse experienced such unity and commitment in war time. A War Relief Fund was established by local churches and organisations working together in raising money, food and clothing for local soldiers. The local miners donated 2d per £ from their wages for as long as the war lasted. The hospital played a major part in the war effort acting as a recuperation hospital for hundreds of wounded servicemen. In fact this is where my mother-in-law May Mair met her husband Pat Murray during the Second World War when he was convalessing. Concert parties were a regular occurrence here during both wars, also at the Public Hall and the Bowling Club. The Rex Cinema formed a committee during World War II, contributing a great deal of money to the war effort.

Food rationing took place in the village during the end of the First World War from around June 1918. This of course was common during the 1940s. The Womens Voluntary Service was responsible for organising food and aiding domestic problems. During the evacuation of the cities in the Second World War the W.V.S. along with the Red Cross and hospital staff, assisted the mass reception of evacuees to the village.

Unlike the war before, German bombers were a constant threat and so the ARP was formed, organised by Dr. Murray. John Johnston was the local warden who made sure that there was a total blackout whenever the threat was present. He was aided by Special Constables Willie Millar and Jack McKinnon, working twelve hour shifts, policing the village. Although no bombs are recorded as falling on the village, it has been noted that a farmer near Goslington saw bombs dropped close at hand, presumably to lessen the load of the German aircraft en route home, after bombing the Clyde. These craters are said to still be in evidence today.

In 1941 an Army Cadet Force was established, with the objective of training youths for military service after school. The Local Defence Volunteers were also formed to prevent the threat of invasion should it occur. The L.D.V. later became known as the Home Guard. During the war Canadians were billeted at Stonehouse Hospital for some time, and Americans are said to have been stationed at Cot Castle.

Alec Torrance

One of many men of notability in the village, during the Second World War was Flight Lieutenant Alec Torrance, of Meadowside Cottage, Lockhart Street. Alec joined the R.A.F.V.R. (Royal Air Force Voluntary Reserve) in 1939, previously being employed as a compositor with the *Hamilton Advertiser*. Alec learned to fly a range of fighter aircraft and was part of the famous 137 squadron flying the 'Whirlwind' bombers on sorties, attacking enemy positions, supply routes and shipping.

In 1941 he sustained burning injuries overseas but was able to resume active service only a few months later, after recuperating in Gibraltar. Based primarily in England during the Battle of Britain, in the later years of the war he was posted to Burma and Thailand as part of a 'Mosquito' bomber crew, attacking Japanese positions.

Some people in the village may remember Alec for his daring swoop under Stonehouse Viaduct, in his 'Whirlwind' during the war years. Unfortunately, Alec was spotted and his number taken and reported to the authorities, and he found himself in trouble with his superiors for his misadventure.

After the war, Alec continued to work in aviation. In 1959 he was Senior Flight Officer with S.A.S. at Prestwick. In 1971 he helped to co-ordinate and plan the route for the famous aviator Sheila Scott, on her journey round the world, via the North Pole. This venture was part of a NASA research project.

Many men from the village took part in the First and Second World Wars, and many were highly decorated. In 1959 Major John Brown, previously of 60 Camnethan Street, was awarded an MBE for his service during and after the war in Malaya and the Mediterranean with the 'Green Berets' and 3rd Commando Brigade.

A.F.W 4026.

Certificate of Proficiency
HOME GUARD

On arrival at the Training Establishment, Primary Training Centre or Recruit Training Centre, the holder must produce this Certificate at once for the officer commanding, together with Certificate A if gained in the Junior Training Corps or Army Cadet Force.

PART I. I hereby certify that (Rank) Pte. (Name and initials) McInnes, G.,
of "C" ~~Battery~~ Company 4th Lanarkshire ~~Regiment~~ Battalion HOME GUARD has qualified in the Proficiency Badge tests as laid down in the pamphlet "Qualifications for, and Conditions governing the Award of the Home Guard Proficiency Badges and Certificates" for the following subjects:—

	Subject	Date	Initials
1.	General knowledge (all candidates)	30 Jan 44	
2.	Rifle	"	
3.	36 M Grenade	"	
*4.	(a) Other weapon Sten	"	
	~~(b) Signalling~~		
*5.	(a) Battlecraft, ~~(b) Coast Artillery, (c) Heavy A.A. Bty. work, (d) "Z" A.A. Battery work, (e) Bomb Disposal, (f) Watermanship, (g) M.T.~~	"	
*6.	(a) Map Reading, ~~(b) Field works, (c) First Aid~~	"	

Date 31 January, 1944   Signature _____ Capt.
                                        ~~President~~ Member of the Board.

The reason for the scar

Locally known as 'Flash', (I didn't ask why!) Gavin Stevenson first crossed my path in the Backroad (Crosskeys, Stonehouse) one winter's evening six years ago. With a Murphy's in one hand and Joanna (his geetar) in the other he had his audience captivated with his songs and verse, sung in his native Lanarkshire dialect. His unusual turn of phrase and entertaining lyrics had me conjuring up images of his characters and so it was with this in mind that we would produce a booklet of his work. As one beer led to another, and another, we exchanged names and numbers but when day dawned all records of that night were lost. Our 'Brief Encounter' was to leave a great impression and influence on me for the next six years. It was my interest in his songs and the stories told, that in part, led me to take an interest in the history and background of Stonehouse, culminating in the establishment of the Heritage Group in 1991.

In the Spring of '94 our paths were to cross again at the Glessart Folk Club one cold Tuesday night, when he was to sing 'The reason for the scar'. This song, like so many, stretched the imagination woven by his lyrics. A hidden and untapped talent, Gavin's songs and verse are of local settings, characters and everyday incidents, which are easily related to in his humorous and descriptive writing.

It was to be my pleasure to be able to illustrate these songs, of which, this is only a small selection of his work. Written in our own local dialect his use of words are often 'choice' but always in the best possible taste. I would sincerely recommend you acquire a copy of the tapes that relate to these booklets, not only for the humour but for the history captured in his songs.

I chose this song not only as my personal favourite but because of its connections with the local Territorial Army Force which was so prominent in the village during and after the Second World War.

They had launched him Thomas Watson. Tae his faither he wis "The Brit"
The road through life Tam rummel't, takin heiders intae it
His schoolin had been wasted, he'd struggled baith tae write n' read
Sat haundy so's the teacher could get a good skelp at his heid.

Jist a waste o' boots n' feedin, a' Tam had mastered wis tae spit
Content tae go fur daunners n' tae row amongst the shit
Noo at nineteen, still unflowered and the sole heir tae "The Neuk"
He wis jist a big raw strappin laddie, who wae wemen'd had nae luck
A sight that made them vomit, fae the start his chance'd been nane
Even the rumour "Stallion Watson" Tam had started a' in vain.

His claim tae fame took place wan night no far fae Canderside Toll
Stonehoose wis a toon o' nae distinction where a train'd wance stopped fur coal
He wis oan his nightly daunner roon "The Conner" near the dam
A wee slice oot o' Eden where the weans a' went n' swam
'Twis a place o' peace 'n beauty, though lovers lay in ranks 'n
Mair than wan pair lassie'd been bairnt upon it's banks
It wis a safe reserve fur wildlife n' the damsel flee still wung
Well as long as it jooked the contraceptives the well-aff winchers flung.

Midsummer's night lay close at haun n' the air still held it's heat
There were cushies croonin o' the mood fit music set fur sleep
But that night it wis fair deserted, nae fishers, n' nae weans swam
Fur the TA had posted warnins they'd manoevres at the dam

Jist afore the sodjers got there the bold Tamas came in view
Like an ad fur wacky-baccy or somethin oot the blue
He wis beltin oot a murdered tune wae neither tone nor beat
Roarin like a donkey that had bugger a' tae eat
The big lungs streeched n' strainin till the peace fur miles wis sent
Gi'en it laldy at the chorus n' the bits he really kent.

It took time tae dawn on Tamas that he'd the place a' tae hisel'
He'd tae sit tae dae his thinkin, so he settled fur a spell
But the big heid widnae function er he gied his lug a thump
The big mooth jist hung open as he pondered on a stump
Twis a movement by the brae face that caught his ee ower by the brim
A squad o' bliddy sodjers, heh, and they were headin straight fur him.

Noo the sodjers had permission fae auld McPherson o' the ferm
Tae blaw up twa big tree stumps that stood each side o' the dam
But the captain o' the sodjers had a weakness fur a hauf
And gi'ed them scant instructions jist afore he'd buggered aff
So like lost sheep they proceeded, nane that shair o' the score
Fur not a wan amang them had used dynamite afore n' so
It came as some relief tae see there waitin by their goal
Wis somebody sent tae help them, and tae pu' them oot a hole.

Good evenin sir wan sodjer said n' Tam assessed him as he spoke
"Nae fears o' this yin jumpin me n' whuppin oot ma coke
The cut o' cloth n' manners n' the polish 'n the style
The big high shiny forehead n' the nae-teeth-missin smile, well
Tam's charisma left them breathless, fur fae right there where he sat
He loosed wan mighty spittle that went whirlin like a bat
And yon sodjers watched in wonder at yon big thing flap 'n fa'
And Tam sat twa pun lighter fur the contents o' his craw.

Tam's total ken o' dynamite had left him wae his spit n'
Nae notion o' their mission said "Eh, ye've a right guid night fur it" n'
Here his greetin mair confirmed their hopes his presence there'd been planned
So it wis wae new-found confidence they gi'ed him full command

Tam's interest in their mission grew n' he watched them dig n' plug
And he followed a' the sodjers roon jist like a collie dug.
Gettin caught up in the excitement, Tam decided he wid coax
"Christ wan stick's jist hauf meesures man, get mair oot o' the box"
Be like doddin it wi' yer bunnet, dae it right man, Jeezis Christ n'
He convinced the raw young sodjers who were glad o' his advice.

Weel yin big stump got hauf the box n' it's neebour got the same n'
Across yon dam the wires were ran n' the charges stappit hame
A respectful distance gi'en, faces pressed hard tae the grun n'
Nae conception o; the damage ye could dae wi' fifty pun

When the mud n' mortar landed, Eden valley wis nae mair
Jist a great big gapin crater, hell the glen wis strippet bare
The parks fur miles were mawkit, hauf the braes were in the toon n'
If ye liked wide open spaces, ye'dve found ye'd plenty room.
A dazed young sodjer found his feet n' left a patch o' green
Fur miles aroon the only grass left staunnin tae be seen
He tried his best tae take yon in n' rubbed his mawkit broo
When a voice behind him brought it hame "By Christ ye've din it noo"

The poor sodjer burst oot greetin "But it wis you that telt us how"
"Heh haud on sur" said Tam "That's a guid yin wantin me tae get the row
You're apposed tae be the experts, Hell I'm jist doon a daunner" n'
He buggered aff n' left therm wae "the cock-up o' the Conner".

Well the captain got demoted fur the things that he'd allowed n'
The sodjers got their arses felt n' private parts well chowed n'
It wis thanks tae the description the sodjers a' had gi'ed
That Tam tae this day bears his faither's bootmarks on his heid.

Gavin Stevenson

Stonehouse New Town

On August 1973 Stonehouse was designated to be a 'New Town', receiving a population from Glasgow of 35,000, with the likelihood of an increase up to 70,000. This project would include twenty five primaries, six secondary schools and the reintroduction of the railway line to Stonehouse.

The purpose of new towns was to accommodate the population living in sub-standard and overcrowded conditions. Despite the decrease in the growth of Scotland's population the number of households have been ever increasing. It was believed by Government that until the social and environmental conditions improved in the urban areas, that the population would continue to leave the big cities, thus the need for new towns, such as East Kilbride, Cumbernauld and Livingston. With this in mind for Stonehouse, the East Kilbride and Stonehouse Development Corporation was formed to create a plan to develop Stonehouse. However, when the newly formed Strathclyde Regional Council was formed it reviewed the plan and decided that the scheme was no longer needed. It was their view that Glasgow should retain its population, with industry directed elsewhere. Thus in the middle of 1977, an Act of Parliament dedesignated Stonehouse as a New Town. However the first phase of the project was carried out with the building of the Murray Drive Estate.[1]

When the New Town proposals were being consulted with the community, they met with mixed feelings, though eighty percent did vote in favour of the New Town, through a referendum at the time. The 'carrot' of industry, better leisure and shopping facilities was a welcome and attractive proposition, but at what cost? Stonehouse had always been a small, thriving close knit community, with many hard working organisations, working together in providing the village with many recreational pursuits and community support groups. One of the villages attractions to residents and 'incomers' is the community spirit and character, where every face is familiar and news travels fast! The New Town, in my opinon, would have threatened this 'community togetherness'.

Many households and farms would have been compulsory purchased to build roads and housing developments. If we think our village is suffering from traffic congestion now, what would the effects on our 'conservation area' and environment have been if a population of 70, 000 were to have come to our village. And what of our Gala Day, Agricultural Fair and Heritage Group, would they have still been here? I doubt it. Do we really want another 'roundabout city' like East Kilbride? The village is constantly under threat of suburban development in what is an area of outstanding natural beauty. The tranquil winding River Avon is freedom on our doorstep, an education and haven for our children to learn from, and explore.

Reference: 1 New Towns

Stonehouse has the potential to expand and prosper within, developing our industry and residential capacity without expanding into our greenbelt. With the first phase of the bypass complete the village can now look forward to a redeveloped village centre within the conservation area, making Stonehouse an attractive location for potential residents and small businesses to locate themselves. Above all we must endeavour to preserve our village's community spirit and character, and provide future generations with a sound economic base and healthy environment to live in. Stonehouse's main employer at present is the hospital providing work for five hundred and fortyy eight staff, around one hundred and fifty of whom live in the village. Unemployment is generally in line with most other villages of a similar size. Unfortunately, apprenticeships are almost a thing of the past with many children opting to go to college or university for further education. There are several large employers of note in the village, including Whitelaw Buses and Wilson Builders, both of whom trade from the Lochpark Industrial Estate.

In an era of large discount stores, supermarkets and purpose built shopping centres, many small rural traders must be suffering from this new approach to shopping facilities. Many shops have come and gone in Stonehouse over the years, of which old Harry McFarlane could name every last one! One of my favourites, and I expect for many others would be 'Graces' (Hamilton) in the Trongate. Trading in household goods and bric-a-brac, the shop is a treasure trove of this that and the other. As a child my memories of shops are confined to one 'Susie's Sweetie Shop' (Susan Sorbie). It was situated in the now demolished tenement, across from the co-operative in King Street. This shop is my only memory of pre-decimalisation, spending my 'thrupenny bit' on lucky bags, liquorice, sherbert dips and Parma Violets. This shop was not only a great loss to myself, but to hundreds of other children who kept our local dentist in great demand.

Born and brought up in Stonehouse, I have experienced in a short time many environmental, economic and structural changes to our village. Primarily a commuter village, housing developments at Murray Drive, West Mains, East Mains, Kittyfell, Muirhead, Crow Road and Boghall have provided housing for an ever increasing population. Unfortunately, leisure facilities are few in comparison to other towns nearby. Parks proposed for Patrickholm and West Mains were never completed, and we have seen over the past thirty years a gradual decay in the condition of our once majestic Public Park. In days of old the park was the holiday and daytrippers' destination for travellers from all over Lanarkshire. This popular tourist attraction of the past has sadly been allowed to lose its attractive and colourful appearance. Due to vandalism we have lost the bandstand tearoom, the public toilets, the boating pond and seating throughout the park. This plague of vandalism has also resulted in severe damage to the fountain commemorating the opening of the park in May 1925 by Alexander Hamilton. Despite this, we have seen some advances in the last few years by way of a new all weather tennis court and an ash running track at the upper end of the park. The park with all its problems, still commands one of the most scenic views of the Avon Valley.

Probably the most common recreational pursuit is 'television', transmitting to ninety nine percent of the population. Whether this form of communication media is good or bad is open to debate, but what is certain, is that, linked with video, TV has revolutionised home entertainment to the point of almost being an addiction. In an era of vast technological advances, computers have become an integral part of everyday life, and the constant demands to obtain the latest technology have put great financial restraints on society. We appear to be in an age where power, possession and wealth have taken precedence over happiness, health and contentment. Fortunately Stonehouse has a thriving social calendar, and a host of clubs and societies providing a wide range of support and leisure pursuits.

Stonehouse is also fortunate to have a well attended and organised Community Council, which deals with many topical issues, and represents the village with its grievances and recommendations. Like so many voluntary organisations it is a thankless task, where members of the community give up their personal time to fight for the rights of the residents of Stonehouse, and a better environment for us all to live and work in.

Stonehouse like everywhere else suffers from ever increasing crime, especially house break-ins and car theft. In the past Stonehouse has been seen as easy prey, due to its rural setting, but with resources being targeted here in the past few years the crime rate has slowly been addressed, and has, as a result, reduced. Crime has always been present as far back as records show, but what is alarming is the nature of the crimes taking place today, previously rarely heard of. Violence, drugs, vandalism and the occasional shooting are all crimes of particular threat to our society, for which there appears to be no apparent solution. Social behaviour, even in the past ten to fifteen years has changed, regarding alcohol in particular. Children will always venture to experience what they are told not to do, and always have, but attitudes and respect for the law has changed. When I was a young teenager, we would take 'oor cerryoot' down to the railway line or drink in the seclusion of the woods, for fear of detection, whereas now teenagers will openly drink in the street without thought for what others think. Why this happens, and what the solution is, is unclear, but it appears that the problem will get worse before it gets better.

The Heritage Group

How the Heritage Group was formed was, accidental. It all transpired during an art exhibition in St. Ninian's Church, in May 1991, where I met Dr. David Duncan who told me that he had been given by Mr and Mrs Mason of Carluke, a set of two hundred and fifty glass slides from the turn of the century. David told me of the excellent condition of the slides and asked if I would know of anyone who could assist in putting on some sort of show exhibiting the slides in the village. I told him of my personal interest in local history and we agreed to organise a meeting in the Public Hall, to which we invited members of the community to attend.

From this meeting emerged a team who decided to establish a group to raise funds and organise the display. The first meeting was attended by the following people; John Young, Helen Murray, Ken Maclean, Ian Baker, Tina Jordan, and Lindsay Greenock with apologies from Dr. David Duncan, John Gavin and Pat Whelan (Community Education). The group was initially to be called Stonehouse Heritage Trust, but the abbreviated SHT for short was thought inadvisable and thus on September 1991 was formed as Stonehouse Heritage Group. Dr. David Duncan was elected as the first chairman and led the group to a highly successful, first exhibition entitled 'Lets go to the Stanes' in September 1992, highlighted by a display of a Victorian school room.

Since that day the Heritage Group has grown from strength to strength, with exhibitions annually in St.Ninian's Church. In 1993 the weaving industry was exhibited and in 1994 the Roman influences in the village were highlighted.

Throughout the years the group have built up an extensive resource library of information and family history data which is all recorded on computer. The interest generated in the village and indeed from all round the world has been encouraging and supportive of the group's work and aims. Working with the elderly, young adults and children of the village they have striven to inform, educate and provide a wealth of knowledge compiled for those wishing to research their ancestors and background. In recent years the group have been actively involved in many issues of concern within the community such as opencast mining, our environment and the village centre plan. Probably the most satisfying and worthwhile projects undertaken have been the restoration of Stonehouses historical sites such as St. Anthony's Well, the graveyard and the gable end of St.Ninian's Kirk. The principal objective at present is to obtain premises to enable the group to provide a focus for research and to act as a resource base for educational support material on the historical background of Stonehouse, and provide a permanent exhibition space for the community to visit. This objective is being actively pursued by the group, whose membership is wide ranging from the early 20s to the late 70s. It is encouraging for the future of the group, though I often wonder how the group are going to attract 'new blood' with statements on our minutes such as "Point 12. History of Fishing—So far Douglas Torrance has renovated an old fishing rod and Joyce Barraclough said that she has lots of photographs of dead fish if we were interested in them!"

The eternal recording of our history is a long way from being complete, but the foundations have been laid for future generations to carry on the work the group have achieved to date.

Bleau's Map 1596

Wha's like us?

The Pools of the Avon

1. Big Lynn
2. Garden Hole
3. Wee Lynn
4. Dreepin Rock Pool
5. Dingwalls Hole
6. Gannister Hole
7. Geordie Nicols Hole
8. March Hole
9. Mill End Hole
10. Washing Green Hole
11. Maid Hole
12. Big Sandy Hole
13. Cut Wood Flat
14. Old Mans Hole
15. Cander Water Hole
16. Black Tub
17. Tods Table Pool
18. Millers Hole
19. Sunny Warm Pool
20. Ritches Dam
21. Yellows Pool
22. Doo Flight
23. Viaduct Pool
24. Todly Well In
25. Bilin Pat
26. Sandwheel
27. Racing Board
28. Park Pool
29. Hazel Hole
30. Securin Pool
31. Reids Haugh
32. Swallow Brae Hole
33. Graveyard Hole
34. Scatter Crag
35. Allans Burn
36. Millholm Pool
37. Allans Haugh
38. Hunterlees Pool
39. Horse Pool
40. Avonholm Flat
41. Blaze Bing Hole
42. Cot Castle Hole
43. Lime Kiln Hole
44. Iron Brig Hole
45. Puddock Hole
46. Keirs

Wha's like us?

Place Names

In Robert Naismith's book he tried to explain many of the unusual and old place names of, and around, the parish. I have tried here, to further his research, deciphering more of our street names, with some going back as far as 1596. This has been done through Atlas, Bibles, Gaelic, Scots, French and English dictionaries. By breaking down the names it is often easier to understand their origins. Some place names however such as 'Kinghahoo' are either too obscure or old, that I could find no explanation for their existence.

Blinkbonny	Bell o' the manse
Ca' fauld	Cow fold
Todstable	Tod's table, where a *tod*, (Fox) is said to have hidden from a pack of pursuing hounds.
Spion Kop (Colliery)	Battle during Boer war
Garibaldi Gates	Italian hero who fought to unite Italy in the mid nineteenth century
Corncockle Tree	This name derives from the Cairncockle mound on the Blackwood Road and has nothing to do with corn.
Couplaw	*Coup;* a rubbish tip, fall, buy or exchange *law;* conical hill, isolated, an artifical mound
Linthaugh	*lint;* a flax plant *haugh;* a piece of level ground on the banks of a river
Holm	*holm;* a stretch of low lying land beside a river
Hazeldean	*hasel, hasil, hazel;* an area covered in hazels *dean, dene;* a local designation (possibly ministers residence)
Munkstibble	*munk;* a noose, snare, religious preacher *stibble;* a probationary minister in the presbyterian church
Kittyfell	*kitty;* prostitute, bad girl, prison *fell;* skin of sheep, slaughter, measurement of land (possibly a slaughter house?)
Flatterdub	*dub;* a pool, muddy or stagnant water
Watstoun	*toun;* an area of arable land occupied by a number of farmers or tennants, a farm with its buildings and surrounding area -Watt's toun
Crumhaugh	*crumak, crummock;* a shepherds crook
Whinriggs	*whin;* 1. hardrock, 2. gorse *rigg;* a long narrow hill, ploughed strip of land
Corslet	*cors;* to seek, search *let;* hinder, prevent, a gate or hurdle used to stop up a gap in a hedge or a wall
Hosnet	*hosnet;* a small stocking shaped net fixed to a pole, used for fishing in small streams, a trap
Udston	*stoun, ston;* a tree stump or tree left after felling

Tofts	*tofts;* a homestead and its lands
Keaphol	*keep;* fortified house *hol;* shallow
Knocken	*knock;* flax or cloth, grain, barley *knok;* hillock
Elrikhoom	*elrich;* resembling elves, weird, ghostly, strange
Kand	*kand (kaner)*; a person appointed to oversee fishing
Taunaker	*taun;* 100 *aker;* acre
Neuk	*neuk, nook;* a projecting point of land, an outlying or remote place
Chalybeate spring	*chale;* shawl (French) *beate;* happy (French)
	chalet; summer cottage (French) This spring can still be seen seeping from the grass, 10ft away from the burn at the foot of Castlehill. A Chalybeate spring contains water bearing iron salts, from the Greek khalups (steel).
Law Farm	*law;* a rounded conical hill, isolated, a grave mound
Waukmill	*walk, wauk;* a pasture for cattle, to shrink after wetting, to beat or thrash
Gristahil	*grist;* (bring) -grist to the mill, corruption of Gristmill
Korskaha	*korsch;* hollow, cavernous
Mount Pisgah	Originates from the Holy Land in Jordan, north of the Dead Sea. Mount Pisgah is the highest point of the mountains of Abarim. The Israelities, led by Moses, reached "'the valley lying in the region of Moab by the top of Pisgah which looks down upon the desert" (Canaan) Nos. 21:20
	Could it be that Ninian (like Moses), in coming from the west to our parish, looking down on 'the promised' land, had the idea of establishing a Christian community? A romantic theory perhaps, but doubtful.
Sodom Hill	Again from the Holy Land. Sodom was the chief city in the Plain, on which the Lord "rained brimstone and fire" (Gen. 19:24-5). Sodom is said to be on the southern border of the land of Canaan, but no evidence has been found of its existence. On the southern shore of the Dead Sea, a hill of salt is recorded as Mount Sodom.
	Hear the word of the Lord, you rulers of Sodom!
	Give ear to the teaching of our God,
	you people of Gomorrah! (Issiah 1:10)
Slaeholm	So called on account of the braes here being covered with sloes bushes.
Ringwell Gardens	Corruption of 'St. Ninian's Well', sometimes known as Ringans Well
Plotcock Castle	*plotcock;* the devil (remains are still evident today)

Thinacres	Probably from the runrigs, still in evidence near Darngaber 'motte'.
Cat Castle (Coat, Cot)	Naismith suggests that 'Cat' in the English and Gaelic language was the scene of a battle, but I can find no evidence of any battle or any definition of it suggesting so. *cat;* (Gaelic) a potato or corn heap *cat;* (Scots) 'cat and clay'- a handful of straw mixed with soft clay used in the building or repairing of walls or buildings.
Muirhead Drive	From the Rev. James Morehead, ordained in 1760 and probably the last minister to preach in the old kirk.
Kittymuir	Said to be derived from "kirk o' the muir". *muir;* area of uncultivated land
Sutherland Avenue	From one of the original doctors to work at the hospital.

Population changes

1696	872	(272 within village, 19 in the village of Sandford)
1755	823	
1790	1060	(593 within village 467 in the country)
1801	1259	
1811	1655	
1821	2038	
1831	2359	(412 houses)
1841	2471	(116 from Sandford area)
1851	2781	
1861	3267	
1871	3177	
1881	3172	(91 in the village of Sandford)
1891	3398	(115 in the village of Sandford)
1901	3665	
1911	3688	
1921	4202	
1931	3703	(Drop, mainly due to emigration and miners seeking work)
1951	4306	
1981	5171	
1991	5033	

Bibliography

The County of Lanark, The 3rd Statistical Acc. of Scotland	George Thomson	1960
Statistical Account of Scotland	Editor: Sir John Sinclair	1855
New Statistical Account of Scotland Volume	Dawson	1791
The New Statistical Account of Scotland Volume VI	William Blackwood	1831
Notes by the way	A.C.M. Michael	1881
Stonehouse, Traditional and Historical	Robert Naismith	1885
Tributaries of the Avon, Lanarkshire	T.F. Harkness Graham	1931
Scenes of the Avon, Lanarkshire	T.F. Harkness Graham	1930s
Rambles through Lanarkshire	J. Jeffrey Waddell	1911
The Grays of Stonehouse Cross	John Gray	1972
A Contribution to the History of Lanarkshire	J.A. Wilson	
Glasgow and Lanarkshire Illustrated	Pub: Hamilton Herald Co.	
Sherifdoms of Lanark and Renfrew	Hamilton	1710
Lanarkshire, Prehistoric and Roman Monuments	HMSO	
Statistical History of Scotland	J. H.D. Dawson	1853
Ordanance Gazetteer/ Scotland Volume VI		1882
Ordanance Gazetteer/ Scotland Volume VI		1885
Ordanance Gazetteer/ Scotland Volume VI		1895
Gazetteer of Scotland	A. Fullarton & Co.	1842
Hamilton Advertiser Pictorial Review		1931
Hamilton Advertiser Pictorial Review		1935
The Industrial Archeology of Scotland	John R. Hume	1976
Martyr Graves of Scotland	Rev. John H. Thomson	1877
The District Council, Official Guide		
New Towns (Scotland) Act. inc. Report on New Town Plan	HMSO	1974
Glassford the Kirk and the Kingdom	Rev. Wm. T. Stewart	1989
Offical guide to Strathaven (inc. Stonehouse)	Fourth District Council	1940s
Scotland's Roman Remains	Lawrence Keppie	1986
Bygone Stonehouse	Richard Stenlake	1994
Lanarkshire Recreational Facilities (Report)	Lanark Education Com.	1948
Hame	George Wilson	1969

The Roman Occupation of South Western Scotland	S.N. Miller	1952
The Stanis Weavers	John R. Young	1993
Proceedings of the Society of Antiquaries of Scotland		1948-49
Memoirs of the Geological Survey, Scotland (Area IX)		1911/21/25
*Hamilton Advertiser*s of the past	Education Resource Service	
The Lanarkshire Miners	Alan B. Campbell	1979
Medieval and Religious Houses of Scotland	I.M. Cowan	
Sweet Believing (Covenanters)	Jock Purves	
The Historical Sites of Stonehouse	John R. Young	1994
Stonehouse: A History in the Press	John R. Young	1994
The Stanis Covenanters	John R. Young	1994
The Lanarkshire Annual		1928
Scots Dictionary		
Atlas of the Bible	John Rogerson	1985
The Archaeological Encyclopaedia of the Holy Land	Avraham Negev	1986
New Towns	Osborn & Whittick	1977
White Star Line (Merchant Fleets No.19)	Duncan Haws	
Passenger Liners of the World since 1893	Nicholas T. Cairns	
A History of the Scottish Miners	R. Page Arnot	1955
The Surnames of Scotland	George F. Black	1946
Whirlwind	Victor Bingham	1987
Larkhall: A historical Development	Jack McLellan	1979
A Short History of Gavin and Rosanah Jack, etc.	Jordan T. Jack	1994
FlyPast (August & October)	Ken Ellis	1994
Roads and Bridges of Lanarkshire	T. U. Wilson	1951
Townhead School Logbooks	Headmaster	
A Village at War	John R. Young	1995
Middle Ward of Lanarkshire Minutes		1900
County Council Medical Reports		
Stonehouse Parish Parochial Records	Rev. Foyer	1696
Census Records		1841,81,91

Illustrations

Cover	St.Ninian's old kirk c.1917 (with Grave digger Johnny Bruce)
Title page	Illustration by author
Page 15	Celtic gravestone in St.Ninian's graveyard 1994
Page 16	Gable end of old St.Ninian's kirk 1994
Page 17	Pewter 'tappit hens' c.1760
Page 18	Stan howse kerk pewter plate c.1760
Page 19	Communion tokens
Page 23	Double Dykes from Sodom Hill 1995
Page 24	Roman Road towards Tanhill 1994
Page 26	Food vessel from Patrickholm cist c.2000 BC
Page 27	Glesart Stanes near Avonholm 1994
Page 28	Cloxy Mill on the Avon 1994
Page 30	Illustration by author
Page 31	Bandstand in Alexander Hamilton Memorial Park 1992
Page 32	Box Office in Rex Cinema c.1950
Page 33	Lighting mount in foyer of Rex Cinema 1994
Page 33	The Homerick
Page 34	Rex publicity advertisement
Page 34	Interior of Rex Cinema c.1950
Page 36	Elizabeth Millar Spinning c.1900
Page 37	Beamers in Camnethan Street c.1900
Page 40	Tramping the blankets c.1900
Page 41	Twisting water from the blankets c.1900
Page 46	Miner extracting coal from Canderigg colliery c.1950
Page 50	Broomfield colliery pre1914
Page 51	Ploughman's lunch
Page 52	Blacksmith plying his trade c.1900
Page 53	Manager John Borland at entrance to kiln at tileworks c.1900
Page 54	Station master at railway station
Page 56	Train near Broomfield colliery pre1914
Page 57	Motorised vehicle c.1900

Page 59	Historical arms of the martyr Patrick Hamilton	
Page 64	Archibald Mathies c.1944	
Page 66	Memorial stone of James Thomson in St.Ninian's graveyard 1994	
Page 68	Grave stone from Cadzow Street graveyard, Hamilton	
Page 71	Old Parish church, New Street c.1900	
Page 72	Hamilton Memorial Church 1954	
Page 73	Building of St.Ninian's church c.1895	
Page 75	Woodwork class at Greenside school pre1914	
Page 78	Class at Townhead Street school pre1914	
Page 79	Curling at Tilework park c.1900	
Page 80	Stonehouse Violet, possibly at Newfield pre1914	
Page 81	Hugh Burns tending his bees 1994	
Page 82	Children fishing for minnows in Avon c.1900	
Page 85	Grossyett knowe on Spittal Road 1994	
Page 86	Stonehouse Pipe Band c.1950	
Page 87	Sir Harry Lauder at Public Hall c.1944	
Page 89	Tofts Farm, site of present hospital c.1900	
Page 92	Blood stone in St.Ninian's graveyard 1995	
Page 95	Illustration by author	
Page 96	Plasterers portrait c.1900	
Page 97	Woman feeding pigs from kettle c.1900	
Page 102	Spectacle E'e falls near Sandford 1994	
Page 103	Thomas Wilson J.P. c.1955	
Page 104	Home Guard c.1940	
Page 106	Home Guard certificate	
Page 108	Illustration by author	
Page 110	Illustration by author	
Page 111	Illustration by author	
Page 117	Map Illustration from Bleaus map of Lanarkshire 1596	
Page 119	Map Illustration of Avon pools	
Back Cover	Farm bothy on Udston by Janet Russell	

Acknowledgements

Hugh Burns, Meadowside Cottage
Jean T. Leishman, Lockhart Street
Kit & Jen Small, Swinhill
Jimmy Leggate, Strathaven Road
Gavin Stevenson (Flash), Uddingston
Andrew Clark, Brankston Avenue
Ian Campbell, Mainacre Drive
James Lambie, Newton Mearns
James Naismith Hamilton, Motherwell
Jordan Jack, United States
Mr & Mrs Whitelaw, Queen Street
William Millar, Avon View
Bob Anderson, St. Ninian's Place
Mrs Allan, Strathaven
Mrs McMillan, Strathaven
John Sheeran, Argyle Street
Janet Russell, Strathaven Road
Mr & Mrs Mason, Carluke
John Russell, Hamilton District Planning Department
Alan Mckenzie, Airdrie Weavers Cottage
Richard Stenlake, Ochiltree
Hamilton Public Library
Hamilton Advertiser
Avondale Standard
Mitchell Public Library, Glasgow
Education Resource Service, Lanark Division
St Ninian's Church Board
Congregational Church Board
The Scottish Maritime Museum, Irvine
Stonehouse Heritage Group

Thanks also to George McInnes, Hugh Murray, Wee Jimmy Anderson and the late Robert Naismith, for inspiration and motivation in writing this book, and a special thanks to my mother for financing this publication, without which, this book would not have been possible